Myers Corners Road

A Short Story Memoir

Richard Buonforte

A Note and Notice from the Author

Thank you for being here in this present moment, you that view these lines on an electronic screen or that hold this book in your hand, printed on paper, a piece of flattened tree, once rooted in the earth, reaching toward the sun. I sincerely hope you will enjoy your journey as you travel down Myers Corners Road, imagining my memories. I dedicated more than two years of my life to this work, hundreds and hundreds of hours of my time. If you find it worthy of your time and want family members, friends, associates, and acquaintances to enjoy it also, please remember that it is illegal to duplicate and distribute any part of this work in print, digital, or any other form without written permission from the author. Please encourage family members, friends, associates, and acquaintances to follow your example and pay the modest amount requested to purchase their own individual copy.

ISBN-13: 978-1542592826
ISBN-10: 1542592828

For my beloved parents and my precious posterity

Contents

A City Boy in the Country

God's country—that's what my mother and our concerned relatives call it, but they mean devoid of civilization, godforsaken. For a city boy in the country, it means a mysterious palpable presence, in the sky and clouds, in the hills and woods, in the rocks and trees, in the ponds and lakes, in the streams and rivers and waterfalls, in the rabbits and deer, in the pheasants and frogs, in the cows and chickens, in the farms and orchards—God's wild country everywhere, a heavenly landscape that continues to call me homeward. I love growing up in this pleasant, peaceful place. Here is where I awaken, where I first feel the creative energy of the earth, where I first hear her humming, crying, sighing, singing songs of sorrow and joy, loneliness and love, death and life. Here is where my attitudes take root, where my values find form, where my body, mind, heart, and soul begin to grow and to take shape. Here is where I experience the influential events that make up this vital episode of my early life on earth.

~*~

We move to Myers Corners Road in June 1961, the summer before I turn nine. We go from our cramped old apartment above my grandparents on East 17th Street in Paterson, New Jersey, to a new four-bedroom house in Wappingers Falls, New York; transported from factories and city streets to the pastoral Hudson Valley, from playing on dirty urban sidewalks to the worthwhile work and leisure we find on a three-quarter-acre parcel of rural land.

I first become acquainted with the area around our new house the day I ask my four-year-old brother, Henry, if he wants to go for a walk. We don't even bother to tell anyone we're leaving, we just set out for a stroll. Before long we're not in Kansas anymore. We've wandered into unknown territory, and there's no yellow brick road to guide our footsteps. We're going to need heart, brains, courage, and heavenly help to get back home. And we'll need to let the land lead the way.

"Are we lost?" my tired little brother asks every so often. I don't want him to get scared and I'm not sure I can handle it if he does, so I tell him if we just keep walking we'll be home soon. We walk for hours, until we travel a long way in a big circle and eventually end up back at the house, back where we belong. We find my frantic mother beside herself with worry. Mom grew up riding city buses and never learned to operate an automobile, so she was stuck at the house, helpless, anxiously awaiting our return, on and off the phone with my father, who is away at work with our nine-passenger Ford station wagon.

"Where have you been?" She sounds angry but relieved.

"We went for a walk."

"Where?" she asks, still annoyed, and exasperated.

"Just down the road."

I guess I don't fully appreciate the problem—not that I'm not paying close attention to our conversation, which now includes a number of Mom's familiar phrases: "God Almighty. Are you out of your mind? I was fit to be tied. For crying out

2

loud—you ought to have your head examined." I never repeat this reckless boyhood blunder, but decades later I do have my head examined by a qualified professional, what he calls a checkup from the neck up, and he finds nothing. Still I admit I continue to enjoy long walks, unlike my younger brother Henry, who seldom wanders away from his house on foot, even half a century later.

A House in The Country

Dad builds much of our new house on Myers Corners Road by himself, after work and on weekends, while we're all still living in New Jersey. Fashion Screen Printing—the company where he went to work after quitting school at sixteen—has already relocated, occupying an ancient factory on the outskirts of Wappingers, not too far from the falls. Much younger than many of his men but respected as a hard worker and skilled craftsman, Dad already has eighteen years on the job and serves as shop foreman, a position worth keeping even if it means moving to upstate New York, to God's country.

Dad hangs sheetrock; installs siding, doors, hardwood floors and baseboard, sinks and toilets, cabinets and countertops; and paints inside and out. Our sources of energy and our utilities are all onsite, except for electricity. We have our own well for water, drilled deep to reach the cold, delicious liquid trapped between layers of ancient shale. Underground leach fields loaded with smooth round stones filter the dirty water from our sinks, tubs, showers, and washing machine. Our toilets empty into an underground concrete cesspool. Our furnace burns oil stored in a five-hundred-gallon tank buried in the backyard. Our water heater is fueled by bottled gas, the tanks connected at the back of the house. And the signal to our black-and-white television is picked up by an antenna attached to the top of our roof.

A sickly child when we lived in the city, afflicted with asthma, a lack of appetite, and an aversion to vegetables and legumes,

3

I'm still small and weak when we first move to the country, ill prepared for strenuous yardwork, which I find difficult and discouraging. As the oldest son, Dad expects me to help him fill the leach fields with stones and cover them and the concrete top of the cesspool with fill dirt and topsoil. I'm too weak to move more than a child-sized portion, and I'm unable to push the wheelbarrow without tipping over unless it's almost empty. Dad rakes and shovels an entire pile of gravel or dirt while I make my few measly offerings. Mom reminds Dad that I'm still only eight years old. Dad went to work on an actual after-school job when he turned ten, so he has higher expectations; but he backs off a bit anyway to appease Mom.

I also help plant grass seed, bushes, and a maple tree in the front yard. Sadly, heavy rains wash away much of the topsoil before the grass can grow—disturbing for Dad, who grew up during the depression and deplores waste. We replant but can't afford to replace all the lost dirt, leaving the front yard with a steep slope that makes it difficult for me to push the lawnmower up and down the hill. During the summer months, I mow the grass every week or two, usually after Dad reminds me, a chore I find dull, the loud engine disrupting my daydreams. In the wintertime, I help shovel snow from our unpaved and deeply-rutted driveway, which runs from the road to the house, a half-acre back and a big challenge.

~*~

A fierce blizzard is blowing, the wind freezing cold, and you can hardly see your hand in front of your face. Dad doesn't give a damn. All he knows is he had better get to the shop in Wappingers and he doesn't have time to fool around. He's throwing snow left and right like he's John Henry racing the steam drill in a contest between industrial technology and good old-fashioned, back-breaking, muscle-straining toil; only Dad's just plain Henry going like a house on fire, nothing to prove, just tons of heavy snow to move. Robert and Little Henry have also come to help, but our youngest brother Kenneth is safe inside with our mother and our older sister Donna, missing out on a truly educational experience.

Dad's going full bore, busting his hump, but he's still able to shout out instructions, the wind so loud I can hardly hear him: "Lift with your legs, not your back." The wet snow is already ankle-high on Dad and calf-high on me and a shovelful weighs as much as I do. Watching out of the corner of his eye, Dad calls out encouragement whenever I stop to catch my breath, a foreign concept in his hard-working world: "Are you gonna lean on that shovel or what?" And when I'm out of energy and can't continue: "You gonna work or rest?"

Fifty-five years later, I truly enjoy shoveling the large parking area and the 225-foot driveway that leads from my house to the street, turning down offers from neighbors with noisy four-wheelers and snowblowers in favor of fresh air and exercise. Besides, I have Dad's help—although he only watches now, having passed over to the other side not long before I bought an acre lot in Springville, Utah. I believe Dad likes what he sees: I lift with my legs, I don't lean on the shovel, and I seldom stop to catch my breath. But I can't say I followed in my father's bigger footsteps. I doubt that when my name is mentioned people say I'm the hardest worker they've ever seen, words I've heard about him all my life.

~*~

Mom doesn't shovel driveways, but she eventually earns her driver's license so she can go to work and so she won't be stuck at the house, although she never becomes what you would call a good driver. She has a heavy foot, a natural tendency to put the pedal to the metal, which is why years later our teenage friends nickname her Leadfoot. Alas, dear Leadfoot's lead foot led to a couple of crashes, accidents that leave me a lifelong defensive driver, reserved, cautious, and careful to a fault. There's the pitch-dark night we're coming up Myers Corners Road in her now classic 1961 Chevy Impala convertible, white with a fiery red interior, Mom running a tortuous passage of twisted turns like she's Mario Andretti driving the Grand Prix; only she fails to keep the car on the road and crashes into the old barbed-wire fence that borders the apple orchard. She's surprised, mystified, and annoyed. The county eventually bypasses that section with a new stretch of straight road, renaming the previous pathway Old Myers Corners Road. Unaware of our adventure, they leave nothing to mark the site, no commemorative plaque, nothing at all in honor of Mom's mishap.

Worse yet is the time we drive to Wappingers to get groceries at the Grand Union. Pulling into a parking space, Leadfoot leans too heavy on the gas pedal and the car rolls out of the parking lot and onto the sidewalk, headed toward Route 9, the widest and busiest street in town. Instead of stepping on the brake, Leadfoot panics and does what comes naturally—puts the pedal to the metal. Our car barrels across two lanes of traffic, knocks off another driver's front bumper, and heads straight for the service station across the highway. The good news is that Mom manages to miss the gas pumps. The bad news is that our local mechanic parked a recently repaired vehicle alongside the front of his shop, all ready to return to its owner. Mom hits the other car so hard she rams it sideways into the shop, causing a noticeable crack down the front of the cinder-block building. Mom is finally stopped by her steering wheel; she isn't seriously injured, but she's unable to move without pain for several weeks. The mechanic is astonished. I don't know if his customer is equally impressed with Mom's maneuver when he comes to pick up his smashed car.

A Leisurely Life

Once we're finally settled in, my early life on Myers Corners Road remains rather undemanding. The area around our house consists of mostly open land, where a boy's body and heart and mind can wander, carefree, unfettered and uncluttered. In the summertime and afterschool and on weekends, I occupy many leisurely mornings, afternoons, and evenings in silence and in solitude. I roam around outdoors, breathing the fresh, fragrant breath of trees, dreaming, musing on the mystery and meaning of life. I lounge on the ground and gaze at clusters of countless stars or stare at huge, billowy, shape-shifting clouds, floating across an endless ocean of air. I sit on the front stoop and watch an occasional car whiz by, wondering where they're coming from and where they're going. And I ride up and down the hills on my dark green and cream-colored Schwinn bicycle, the world flying past my face, warm and friendly.

My brothers and I crawl into the empty cardboard boxes left behind by the refrigerator, the stove, and the washer and roll each other down the hillside behind our house. We play with our Tonka trucks. Vroom. Vroom. Vroom. We play army with our toy machine guns and Dad's old army belt and canteen, the Americans against the Germans or the Japs. Hrrt-hrrt-hrrt-hrrt-hrrt-hrrt-hrrt. And we wrestle. I lie on the ground, three little brothers on my back, then flip over and pin them all at once. This won't last long since soon they'll be too big for me to manhandle. We play football in the fall and softball in the spring and summer in our big backyard. Later we shoot marbles and flip baseball cards under the carport Dad builds to protect our cars from the harsh winter weather. We collect caterpillars into a cardboard box and then set the sides of the box on fire with a cigarette lighter—until my nightmares nip this bad idea in the bud, saving countless caterpillars from my fiery dreams.

For a rather long time, our only neighbors are Lou and Marie Gagarono and their daughter Marian; and Mrs. Supris, who lives farther down the road toward town. On the other side of Myers Corners Road, across from our house, there are only woods and a few houses up a little hidden lane, where we aren't allowed to venture. The only other houses are farther away and also out of sight, blocked by rolling hills, big trees, and thick bushes, scattered down Dogwood Hill Road, Degarmo Hills Road, All Angels Hill Road, and Top O' Hill Road. Behind our backyard, the land is unoccupied by people all the way back to Gold Road; all the way to where we eventually find wild raspberry and blackberry bushes—and poison ivy and poison sumac, whose mere touch makes me miserable, provoking an intense allergic reaction. But Mom soothes my suffering with a home remedy: she dissolves some cornstarch in freezing cold water and gently applies the mixture to my face and arms with cotton balls.

Within walking distance of our house there's a small dairy farm with a little pond full of big bullfrogs. One day my brothers and I bring a foot-long friend home and introduce him to our older sister while she's relaxing in our small, two-foot high swimming pool. But it turns out she isn't the kiss-a-frog kind of girl and doesn't appreciate our earnest efforts to bring a little romance into her lonely life. Beyond the dairy farm there are only woods and a stream and Strigham's Country Store, where Mom and Dad take us for mouth-watering, homemade ice cream on occasion. I ride the school bus through this rough countryside, staring out the window at the wild scenery, moving slowly toward Hopewell Junction but stopping at Fishkill Plains Elementary School, where I finish the fifth and sixth grades, three long miles from home.

Down Myers Corners Road in the other direction is a larger pond; beyond the pond the volunteer fire department; then the apple orchard, where we pick apples by the bushel in the fall; after that the little farm where we buy our eggs; and still closer to town, a small country restaurant that makes tasty rotisserie chicken—owned by an older Jewish couple from Brooklyn— where Mom and Dad take us to eat out from time to time; and finally the village of Wappingers Falls, where we sometimes go to St. Mary's on Sundays or to the old Catholic monastery in the hills behind the village, with its awe-inspiring a cappella choir.

During the wintertime, we ice skate after school in the bigger pond if the weather's cold enough for a safe, solid freeze; and on the weekends, we go to nearby Lake Oniad, a larger location that draws more skaters, both kids and adults. When we can't ice skate, we sleigh down the hill on the side of our house. Or we have snowball fights until one of the younger kids cries, or until our woolen gloves are soaked, or until too much snow slides down our shirts or socks or up our sleeves. Then we head inside, bringing Mom a major mess of wet winter clothes.

~*~

Mom and Dad work endless hours to give us things we don't deserve and they can't afford, but that help us keep our noses clean, as Dad would say. And after a while, they earn enough to buy us a swing set and eventually a big aboveground swimming pool. We all help put the pool up in the spring, a real chore, heavy and frustrating work; and we're impatient to see it full of water and ready for fun. When it's time to take the pool down, we all pitch in once more, but it's sad to see the source of our happiness dismantled and stored away for winter, to see the summer end and school begin again.

During the summer months, we practically live in the pool—and everyone survives. We dive off the low ladder and swim across the pool. We play dodge ball and stage chicken fights, trying to knock each other off a large rubber ball held tightly between our locked legs. We have fun. But every so often my sister or one of my younger brothers leaves the pool in tears, and that brings Mom out on the back porch to yell, threaten, or make us come out of the water altogether.

Mom seldom gets in the water without Dad—she's probably too busy washing dozens of dirty towels and wet underwear and bathing suits. But I bet she's also inside basking in her peaceful solitude or catching a nap after her nightshift, until we disturb her with one of our squabbles. When they aren't busy working, and have spare time, Mom and Dad come in the pool with us on weekends. And sometimes they swim alone together after sundown when the air is cool and the water still warm. When we're older, Donna and I are allowed to join them on occasion.

One weekend Dad shows us how to make a whirlpool by walking around the perimeter of the pool together in the same direction, good exercise that also adds to our sense of unity—going in the same direction is not our natural inclination. Once the water is flowing as fast as possible, revolving around its whirling center, we turn and try to walk the other way, the strong current sweeping the smaller children back unless they cling tightly to the side, the adults and taller kids pushing our bodies forward against the rushing water by forcing our feet into the bottom of the pool. Making a whirlpool soon becomes a favorite family activity, but we need Mom's and especially Dad's taller, stronger bodies to get the water going, so whenever they join us in the pool, we immediately begin begging: "Let's make a whirlpool, let's make a whirlpool." We watch and wait while they warm up and enjoy the water for a few leisurely minutes before letting us borrow their bodies for our own fun.

It's my job to take care of the pool. I'm supposed to vacuum the bottom and skim bugs and debris from the surface. I'm expected to test the water, add chlorine and fungicide, and put diatomaceous earth in the filter. I must cover and uncover the pool and flip the ladder up and latch it securely. And I should let Dad know if there are any problems. In turn, he doesn't hesitate to let me know when the surface looks nasty or the bottom sandy, when the water's turning green or feels slimy, or when the ladder's been left down. I don't dare tell Dad I forget to do my work off and on because I'm too busy daydreaming. I know better than to claim that it's not my fault that my younger brothers leave the ladder down. And I keep secret that we boys often use the pool as an outdoor urinal because Mom doesn't want us to track water through the house—although I'm sure she doesn't mean for us to put the silent pee in swimm*p*ing.

I also help Dad backflush the filter whenever it's clogged up, listening to him explain in tedious detail how everything works and learning to stay out of his way, watching and watching out. I learn that you need to prime the pump if you want it to work properly—you need to get the air out of the system. Lost in my own thoughts, I fail to see the life lesson in front of my face, but I'm still young and it will take quite a long time to learn and relearn all the lessons that life here on earth affords when we're willing to cooperate.

Fun and Games

We don't have an indoor pool to keep clean and Mom doesn't let us help with housework, so inside our cozy house it's all fun and games, except when we misbehave. We play games in our cramped kitchen until we're blue in the face or red-faced with frustration, overheated with all-American competitive energy. Usually we play Trouble or Battleship, occasionally Candy Land or Monopoly. Donna always wins at Monopoly, outwitting us with her head for numbers and business. She's always the banker since she's the oldest and we boys don't want to manage the money. We don't really even want to play Monopoly since it takes so long and we never win. We'd rather knock each other's block off with our Rock'em Sock'em Robots or play electric football. Boy, do we love to play electric football—the spring-loaded kicker, the firm cotton football, the deafening motor vibrating the sheet-metal playing field, the tiny plastic players moving every which way but where you want them to go, the yelling and cheering and taunting and arguing.

My brothers and I also like to stage imaginary battles with our dozens of plastic army men and our big G.I. Joe. When we feel real brave, we borrow Dad's wire cutters and inflict an actual injury, maiming a man by hacking off his hand. Maybe we got this gruesome idea from one of Dad's stern warnings: "I'll chop your hands off." We're not sure exactly what he has in mind since Dad's not a surgeon, or a poet, but we know this means he's dead serious and we had better not do whatever we were planning. Or at least we shouldn't get caught—unless we want to see him clarify the blurry boundary between what decades later I would learn to call metaphorical and literal meanings, the line between imaginative semiotic process and actual embodied experience, between the symbolic and the real.

Now and then Mom joins the fun and games, entertaining us with her amazing ability to play Pick-Up Sticks and jacks and to hit a Hi-Li paddleball. We're awkward at jacks—a girl's game anyway—barely able to bounce the little solid red ball and to pick up even one jack before the ball bounces again. But Mom throws the jacks, bounces the ball, and picks up one jack, then two, then three, and on to ten without missing, all in a matter of seconds. And she can hit the hard ball attached to the Hi-Li paddle with a long elastic band more than one hundred times before missing even once, while we manage only a handful of uncoordinated hits.

In our big formal living room, we listen to music on our phonograph, later a Hi-Fi, eventually a stereo with two separate speakers. Until we're teenagers, we listen mostly to Mom and Dad's records: Perry Como, Dean Martin, and other popular Italian-American crooners; and big band music from the forties, Benny Goodman and Glen Miller, with Mom singing along with Rosemary Clooney, Bing Crosby, and the Andrews Sisters, even though she can't carry a tune in a bucket. And we get a big kick out of "Pepino, the Italian Mouse," "Please Mr. Columbus (Turn the Ship Around)," and "What Did Washington Say (When He Crossed the Delaware)?" Mom translates when Lou

Monte's bilingual Washington answers in Italian: "It's cold and I'm hungry." We also enjoy Louie Prima's lighthearted lyrics in "Please No Squeeze Da Banana," an immigrant shopkeeper's complaint about an Irish cop that manhandles the goods on his fruit stand while walking his beat along the city streets:

You touch-a dis, you touch-a dat, you touch-a everyting.
You push-a dis, you push-a dat, you never buy noting.
So please-a no squeeza da banana.
If-a you squeeza, officer please-a, squeeza da coconut.
Squeeza da watermelone.

During the Christmas holidays, it's Gene Autry singing the so scandalous "I Saw Mommy Kissing Santa Claus" and warning us we better watch out, that "Santa Claus is Coming to Town" and he knows if we've been bad or good. And that's a sobering thought at our house, where bad behavior is far too common. When we're more naughty than nice, Dad threatens we'll get a piece of coal in our stockings and reminds us that when he was a kid during the depression, they were lucky to get an orange and a little handful of nuts. But good old Mom and Dad always manage to end up spoiling us with more toys and clothes than they can afford.

When the music moves them and they're in the right mood, Mom and Dad roll back our big living room rug on the odd occasion and polka around the hardwood floor, recalling their carefree days before we were born, when many of their friends were Polish, including my sister's godfather, Freddy Stikvis. We get the impression the folks were a lot of fun in their day, which wasn't all that long ago I guess. Mom and Dad remain sociable while we're growing up and sometimes invite other couples over for a few drinks or for cake and coffee and conversation in our compact kitchen. If I don't interrupt, I'm allowed to listen and learn as adults tell stories and talk about their experiences. And

14

I get a real earful, as my mother would say, dismissed, however, when the conversation becomes too mature.

~*~

After a while, Mom and Dad save enough money for Dad to finish our cold, damp, dark basement. He nails furring strips to the concrete walls and then puts up solid knotty-pine paneling. He lays down asphalt tiles over the cement floor and installs hot-water baseboard radiators. I hand him his tools, materials, nails, and boards. I hold the tape while he measures and marks. And I struggle to keep boards still while he saws and hammers and copper pipes while he solders fittings with a handheld blowtorch. I learn that you should measure twice and cut once and that you should pay attention to what you're doing.

With a finished basement, we have a bigger and better place to play, out of Mom's hair and out of her sight, a place that permits more creativity, like the day I come downstairs to find that Henry has invented an electrifying form of entertainment. He's plugged a loose lamp cord into a live wall socket and he's cutting through the plastic insulation with a pair of Mom's metal surgical scissors. If he had any brains, he'd be dangerous, as she would say. "Look, look at this," he calls out, leaping and dancing a very lively high-step as long streams of orange sparks sizzle through the air.

"You're going to kill yourself," I warn, playing the part of the responsible older brother.

"I'm wearing sneakers," he says, lifting one foot to show off the rubber soles. I shake my head and hope for the best. Lucky for him that he's right and he remains unscathed, kept safe by his trusty Keds—unlike Mom's poor scissors, their steel edges melted by his innovative but insane antics.

To protect Mom's sanity and to keep us out of trouble, Mom and Dad decide to equip our basement rec room with a pool table that they can't afford. I guess they haven't heard the Music Man's warning that once you get a pool table, you've got trouble in River City, but we're not in River City, so it's A-Okay. When we tire of pool, we put the portable Ping-Pong top on the table and go to town. Robert gets so good he puts a pillow on the tile floor and beats us from his knees, blasting Ping-Pong balls past our slow, helpless hands. Whizz. Bang. He's the master of humiliation, a talent he later transfers to tennis and basketball. We also play darts downstairs and nobody ends up at the hospital. But Dad decides that he should protect his beautiful tongue-and-groove paneling from our wayward throws, so he hangs a corkboard on the wall behind the dartboard, although it's unnecessary once we all develop a dead-eye aim.

Years later we band together in the rec room and make noise meant to be music, until poor Mom's prayers are answered and Robert and Henry lose interest in the drums and electric guitar. But by now I have my own room downstairs, where I listen to loud music and play my electric bass guitar through a powerful amplifier and two fifteen-inch speakers. Mom and Dad don't say much, but I imagine that Mom's probably upstairs muttering "Jesus, Mary, and Joseph" under her breath.

And in a little alcove on the far end of the rec room, we absorb an endless stream of television programs, interspersed with advertisements for numerous new products, food for the postwar American mind and new merchandise to suit a modern lifestyle. Despite their farfetched and idealistic angle, these fanciful depictions of our past and present prepare me for future episodes of my own long-running series, for its various twists and turns and ups and downs, including reruns; and teach me to have hope when everything doesn't always work out the way I want; to handle what happens with courage, compassion, and a lively sense of humor, lessons Mom and Dad also quietly display in real life, where everything doesn't always wrap up in thirty or sixty minutes minus commercials.

Fascinating Neighbors

When we first move to Myers Corners Road, we share a party line with our neighbors, Lou and Marie Gagarono, and nosy neighbor Marie likes to listen in on Mom's telephone calls—just to make sure everything's okay over at our house.

"Marie, I know you're on the line because I can hear you breathing."

"No, I'm not," says Marie. Then Mom hears her hang up the receiver. Fascinating.

Marie should work for the federal government, where her ability to eavesdrop and then blatantly deny what she's doing might serve national security. No wonder I still hate talking on the phone and for many years prefer more primitive telephonic technology: two tin cans with a waxed string stretched between them. After all, it's hard to listen in on a tin-can conversation. But this simple device doesn't work well over long distances, so several years ago I finally decided to trade the tin cans for a smart phone, complex equipment with a different disadvantage.

It allows Big Brother, our nosy neighbor, to eavesdrop on our calls—just to make sure everything's okay over at our house.

Lou Gagarono prefers eye-to-eye communication and in-your-face confrontation, and he'd rather talk than listen. He's what my mother calls a bullshit artist, working in the same medium as our advertising agencies, career politicians, and corporate bigwigs. One day Lou comes over to complain that one of us boys made a rude remark about Marie, that she was bending over in their yard and one of us said, "I wish I had a B.B gun." And he wants Dad to give the perpetrator a proper beating. As a responsible parent, Dad's obligated to receive Lou's complaint and conduct a hearing, but he isn't about to let any outsider tell him when to perform his disciplinary duties. That's Mom's job: "Wait till your father gets home." It's also Mom's job to tell Dad when to stop: "That's enough Henry." They're a team—she sics him on us, he does the dirty work, and then she calls him off; except when she can't wait, then she wields her trusty wooden spoon or an old Hi-Li paddle.

Dad prefers to let his belt do the talking, and he's the fastest strap in the east, standing or sitting, two hands or one, at home or on a long trip. Both eyes on the road and one hand on the wheel of our nine-passenger Ford station wagon, he unbuckles his belt and wails away at everyone in the middle seat. No need to worry about who's actually at fault since we're all always guilty of something. His strap isn't long enough to reach the rear seat, but if you misbehave back there, he'll stop the car, get out, and warm up your rear seat. And if you run and think you've escaped punishment when you see him take off his belt at home, think again, think covert action. He'll come up to you two weeks later when you're just sitting there minding your own business and ram an unexpected middle knuckle into your thigh.

"What was that for?" you ask, rubbing your leg.

"You thought you got away with it, didn't you? You thought I'd forget all about it."

In the case of Gagarono v. Buonforte, Dad cross-examines me first since I'm the oldest. I certainly could have made the alleged statement because I do want a B.B. gun and Marie's butt does make a target big enough for a beginner. But I believe one of my bolder younger brothers, Henry or Robert, deserves full credit for expressing the idea so succinctly. Either way, we all want to live to tell the story, so we play dumb and deny any wrongdoing. We shrug our shoulders and shake our heads like we have no idea what Mr. Gagarono's even talking about, like it's all a figment of Marie's overactive imagination. Maybe she's been eavesdropping on too many phone calls or maybe her mind's warped from worrying about national security; maybe she misheard since we weren't on the telephone at the time.

But Lou doesn't have his listening ears on during Dad's interrogation anyway. He's argumentative and out of order, busy trying to influence the judge, jury, and executioner, talking loud and fast and furious, his eyes fixed and glazed, his brow glistening. And he's foaming at the mouth. I can see spots of cottony spit forming between his tense lips, in the middle and at the corners. Fascinating. Also disgusting. Occasionally a spot of spit sprays off in Dad's direction—and Lou's only inches from Dad's face, trying to go nose-to-nose, playing the risky part of Mr. Intimidation. Dad manages to hold his tongue and his temper, but by now he's annoyed and aggravated and feeling defensive, and it's getting louder and louder in our cramped kitchen. My stomach churns and I feel a little lightheaded.

Also fascinating is the casual way Lou interjects swearwords into his utterances, words that begin with the lower letters of the alphabet, a and b and d; and especially the explosive fricative f with its initial puff of noxious air, still a fully-loaded word these days, rarely heard in mixed-company. And then there are the creative combinations, some also employing key letters from the far end of the alphabet: d__ b__, f__ b__, s__ o__ b__, and d__ s__ o__ b__ and f__ s__ o__ b__. It's like he's somehow stumbled upon a new kind of Morse code that generates only words banned by the FCC. His mind trained on truth, justice, and the American way, Dad fails to see a unique opportunity for us to expand our vocabulary. He takes exception to Lou's form of verbal folk art and tells him to watch his language in front of his wife and kids. Unaware of his unconscious habit, Lou blankety-blank denies he's blankety-blank swearing. Fascinating. I suppose he imagines that he's just uttering uh when he pauses to retrieve appropriate terminology from his limited lexicon.

Running out of words, Lou decides he should let his muscles do the talking; he's a master carpenter that saws boards and hammers nails by hand all day long, so why shouldn't he risk entering into the regulatory domain of the New York State Boxing Commission. Seeking justice, Lou leans in and shoves his body against Dad's, from hip to shoulder. Dad braces and shoves back. They're like two big bull walruses maintaining a standoff on a rocky beach. But they lack room to maneuver, jammed between three closed doors in an area barely big enough for a doormat. Scuffling and shuffling their heavy work shoes, they bang into the backdoor behind Lou, bump sideways into the door to my brothers' bedroom, and smack into the door at the top of the stairs that lead down to the basement behind Dad. My pulse counts out the beat while my stomach does the twist and shout with Chubby Checker. I'm worried about what might happen next, afraid my father might get hurt or be embarrassed or get into trouble if he knocks Lou into the middle of next week, as my mother would say.

Despite all of his tough talk and his confident swagger, Lou's sweaty palms show he's about to shit his pants, as my mother would say. Dad's lips, on the other hand, are turning white around the edges, a sure sign he's really mad and you had better watch out buster—Mom tells us afterwards—because all hell's about to break loose. But Dad makes a last-ditch effort to avoid unleashing his anger and bashing Lou's hard head through our solid wooden backdoor. "Louie," he says, "I think we better stop before we do something we'll both be sorry for." Lou's not as dumb as he looks, as my mother would say. A ray of bright light penetrates his muscular mind and he picks up on Dad's warning. Grasping a chance to save his face, he decides to back down and avoid an embarrassing exit through a closed door. He mumbles a conciliatory comment and heads home to his castle, where his wife and precious daughter await the outcome of his diplomatic mission. Mom wisely refrains from saying, "Don't let the door hit you in the ass on the way out."

Dad sits down at the kitchen table, relieved he managed to avoid violence. We rush to his side, proud and chattering about the skirmish, our agitated minds now at ease, but Dad dismisses our boyish banter. He never expresses the idea with words, but Dad's attitude comes across loud and clear: you fight only when absolutely necessary, only when you're willing to kill, and that rules out everything foolish and unimportant, a lesson I fail to learn until after a few of my own unfortunate experiences, a lesson still lost on our federal officials.

~*~

We forget the conflict after a while and our relationship with the Gagaronos soon returns to what passes for normal in our little neighborhood—friendly enough for government work, to paraphrase a popular saying. Some seven years later, Lou and Marie introduce my parents and me to a business opportunity, and we often gather at our area leader's home for coffee and conversation after our weekly recruiting meetings. It's mostly chitchat and stories—but not the story about Dad and Lou's dance in the doorway.

As general distributors, we take turns closing the weekly recruiting meetings—explain the business, relate our so-called personal success story, and try to persuade guests to sign up. When Lou's turn comes, he stares at the audience, his pupils dilated, his face paralyzed, his smile stiff as petrified wood. He loses his language, his memory, and his presence of mind, his speech halting, unfocused, confusing; and his mouth as dry as the Arizona desert where he later goes to live, cottony spit stuck between his taut lips. I doubt that the poor bastard can even remember a damn swearword, although we hope he left that language at his day job.

Lou's stage fright fills the room—so thick you can cut it with a knife and butter it on your bread—and we all pity the poor son of a bitch, especially Marie, who's as uncomfortable in her seat as if she'd been shot in the butt with a B.B. gun. When Lou touches the blackboard, we wonder if he's stumbled upon a new form of finger painting—with perspiration: wet as a washcloth, his hand leaves behind the clear image of a palm and five fingers. Fascinating. At least Lou looks sharp in his shiny white shirt and brand-new olive-green suit. But he also looks like he's about to shit his pants, as my mother would say.

Perfect Circle

I don't dislike Mrs. Mason, my fifth-grade teacher at Fishkill Plains Elementary School, but I don't really like her either. She seems touchy and tired, worn and weary from her work, and unapproachable. She's certainly not like friendly, white-haired Mrs. Freeman, the first-grade teacher who helped button my winter coat at Public School No. 18 in Paterson, New Jersey, her face full of smiles. Or like old Mrs. Schmiefendort, my very first schoolteacher, whose German ancestors gave kindergarten its happy name: child garden. Or like laidback Andy Brubaker, my best friend in the fifth grade, and my bodyguard.

Nearly two years younger and much smaller than all the other boys, I often find myself bullied until Andy takes me under his arm. Put off by his size and strength and perhaps by the unfamiliar farm odors that cling to his clothes, the other boys know better than to tangle with Andy; and to leave me alone now that I'm under his protection, shielded by his big, solid body. But unwary Andy is the one in want of protection today, when he quickly finds himself outmaneuvered by Mrs. Mason, brought down to earth with a thunderous, silent thud.

Mrs. Mason draws a round figure on the blackboard, refers to the object as a circle, and is about to begin her lesson. Impelled by a reckless spasm of temporary insanity or one wild hair or sheer boredom, Andy suddenly interrupts and interjects a correction. "That's not a circle," he announces out of the blue, as if making an astute observation for a sophisticated audience. Mrs. Mason isn't about to brook any bull from Andy, even if his family works on a farm that raises prize-winning Black Angus bulls, and she sure doesn't let his bullshit slide now. She takes his statement as a veiled challenge and summons him to see if he can do better, to come forward and show the class how to draw a perfect circle on the blackboard.

Andy baulks.

Mrs. Mason insists, holding out the chalk.

Andy has really put his foot in it this time. He crosses the classroom like a condemned man climbing thirteen unlucky steps to the gallows, his doom certain. His first irregular shape looks more like a cow pie than a pristine round plane figure whose outer boundary—the circumference—consists of points equidistant from a fixed point—the center. His failure takes all the starch out of his shorts, as my mother would say, but Mrs. Mason demands that Andy take another stab at it. The tip of his tongue in the corner of his mouth, he makes an earnest second effort but ekes out only a woeful, wobbly form, mishandling his tiny piece of chalk like a city boy milking a cow for the first time. Mrs. Mason calls for another attempt, and then another, until Big Andy Brubaker cries out, cowed. "I can't," he bellows, his voice choking, his ears crimson, his face flush and fallen, hot tears sliding down his chubby red cheeks. He lumbers back to his desk, his long walk of shame punctuated with muffled sobs and the sound of shuffling shoes. Our eyes turned down, we sit in stunned silence, scared shitless, as my mother would say.

~*~

I wonder if what happened that sorry day in the fifth grade is why I teach for twenty-six years at a large private university but seldom write on the blackboard and never draw a single circle. I wonder if Andy's humiliation is also the reason that I eschew instructor-dominated lectures and reject the rigid order of rows. Instead, we arrange our desks in a square and sit so we can all see one another and share our responses to thought-provoking readings about our common human condition, each adding a unique contribution to our learning community.

I admit my account of Andy's encounter with Mrs. Mason passes through the filter of a disturbed mind, disjointed by long division and fractured by fractions, my homework a giant mess of mistakes and ugly erasures. My inability to comprehend the drive to divide confirms my natural affinity for the whole, the holy and the healthy. It reinforces my innate inclination toward unity, union, communion, cooperation, and community; and it deepens my strong distaste for disunity, fragmentation, factions, competition, and power struggles—like this one between a boy too big for his britches and a teacher too big for hers.

Lost Leg

Our cramped kitchen feels warm and crowded and full of my parents' quiet compassion and of the heartfelt gratitude of these good people. It's a celebratory occasion. Jimmy Barcocotti has finally recovered from his ordeal and been outfitted with an artificial leg, and he and his wife and their kids have come to visit and to thank my mother and father. Mom helped take care of Mr. Barcocotti while he was in Vassar Hospital, where she works on the night shift as a nurse's aide; and Dad helped make sure he made it there in the first place.

Amid the commotion, Mr. Barcocotti leans across our thick pine kitchen table and looks into my face in earnest, straining to be heard amid the loud chatter of excited voices. "Your father saved my life," he says. I don't know how to respond, so I just sit there, embarrassed and uncomfortable. And I feel awkward about him losing his leg.

"Your father saved my life," he repeats, to make absolutely certain I know how he sees what happened that horrible day.

Dad doesn't disagree with Barcocotti's claim—that would be disrespectful—he just keeps to himself. He recognizes that his actions made a difference, maybe all of the difference, but he wouldn't want anyone to overstate the case, to imply that he's a hero. Whenever Dad tells the story, he's just a regular joe that happened to hear a cry for help; and he regrets that he wasn't able to do more and that Barcocotti lost his leg because of that butcher, that damn doctor.

I've already heard the sad story, how Dad's working down at the shop in Wappingers Falls one day when he hears someone hollering from the unpaved parking area several floors below. "Help... help... help..." At first he figures that it's a bunch of construction workers clowning around and ignores it. But the cries continue to repeat, off and on, on and off, a kind of Morse code embodied in a distant human voice.

"Help... Help... Help... ... Help... Somebody help... ... Help...somebody..."

"That doesn't sound like someone's joking," Dad says to himself. He hurries over to the window to see what's wrong—and there's a man lying on the ground, not far from his dump truck. Dad hustles down to help and he finds Jimmy Barcocotti with a very badly busted leg, the shattered bones sticking out through his torn flesh. Dad runs inside and calls Dr. Silverman for help.

Dr. Silverman has a bad drinking problem, but he's the only doctor in Wappingers Falls. He takes a quick look and decides he should set Barcocotti's mangled leg immediately. When Dad sees the doctor isn't even going to wipe the grit and gravel from the broken bones, he attempts to intervene on Jimmy's behalf. "Shouldn't you clean off all that debris first?" he asks. The insulted and angry doctor shouts for him to shut up and mind his own business and waves him off. Put firmly in his place, Dad joins the worried group of men now gathered to watch what's happening. He's pissed off, "But what're ya gonna do—he's the doctor, right?"

Dr. Silverman doesn't bother to give his patient anything to dull the pain; he just thrusts the broken bones back into the torn leg. Dad says that Barcocotti, the poor bastard, lets out a scream like you can't believe. In my mind, I hear his horrifying howl bounce off the building and pierce the ears and chill the souls of the workers witnessing his torment. And I imagine the shrieking sound crashing to the ground, like shards of shattered glass, splintered artifacts of an unforgettable experience.

~*~

One weekend Dad asks if I want to go down to the shop with him, and I say yeah, sure. We ride quietly along Myers Corners Road in our nine-passenger Ford station wagon, drive through the village to the outskirts of Wappingers Falls, and stop down by the river at the ancient factory now occupied by Fashion Screen Printing. No one else is around, but Dad's the shop foreman, so he has the key to every heavy wooden door in the building, all on a big steel ring that hangs from his belt loop. We head inside and ride an old freight elevator up a few floors. Metal doors drop open and bang shut and clatter open again after the cables crank and creak and slowly haul us upward.

We step out into an enormous room with exposed pipes and heavy electric cables and ductwork running along the high, open ceilings. The cold room is packed with wide tables as long as a Pop Warner football field, covered with white fabric stretched tightly across their width and along their length. Dad grabs one of the large frames leaning against the wall and takes the time to tell me how they screen print tablecloths and other items, using techniques that I learn years later belong to an ancient art. He explains how they pour thick colored inks into the frames and use huge squeegees to push the dense fluid through cutouts in the mesh screens to form decorative patterns on the cloth.

Dad doesn't make a big deal out of what he does, but he seems pleased with his craft, with the skills he first acquired when he quit school at sixteen to help support his family. I don't say much either, other than ask a few confused questions, but I'm impressed with how it all works, a mystery revealed that remains a marvel. I also see that Dad knows every aspect of his trade from start through finish and that he knows how to create useful and attractive products that enhance everyday life and help make holidays special.

While Dad takes care of the tasks he came to accomplish, I walk over to the window and look down at the dirt parking area below, down where Jimmy Barcocotti broke his leg and where Dad might have helped save his life. On our way out of the building, Dad picks up a can of crude petroleum jelly to take home, basically dark amber axle grease. Whenever we have a scratch or a scrape, we smear this unrefined version of Vaseline on the wound, only it works even better, sealing out germs and allowing the injury to heal fully. In my preadolescent innocence, I wonder whether this ointment would have worked its magic on Barcocotti, if a more caring and more competent doctor had used what Dad calls common sense and cleansed the wound and then applied this salve to help save the now lost leg.

Dark Matter

It's as if we've been pulled into the picture tube and we're caught up in a special episode of a popular TV program—and it's definitely not Father Knows Best; it's a nightmare montage that merges the Twilight Zone with Have Gun—Will Travel and The Edge of Night, a somber adult soap opera. Presented without any commercial interruption, this horrifying production takes less than an hour, but its fragmented afterimages and its unnerving influence last much longer, disturbing our already imperfect home and disrupting my already insecure and anxious life. My sensitive mind and tender ten-year-old heart remain unsettled for many years to come.

I'm far too naïve to understand what Dad's worried about or to understand why he even decided to tell us, why he woke up Donna and me and led us to the basement where he could talk to us in private and without waking our little brothers. But he's going on about how he suspects that Mom might be seeing this Black man she works with on the graveyard shift over at Vassar

Hospital in Poughkeepsie. He doesn't say if they're just sharing a cup of coffee during their break or what. But he's determined to find out what's going on and to put a stop to it—not because he's completely paranoid or totally delusional but because he's obligated to protect his family, desperate to defend his marriage.

Dad's really fit to be tied, as my mother would say, filled with frustration fed by fear and shame and concern for family honor. Dead serious, he lets out loud, intense whispers, his hands and arms insulting the air. Confused by this incoherent encounter with an ominous outside world and an alien Dad, Donna and I are weary but wide awake, and we're totally overwhelmed with emotion. Our bodies burst into spontaneous convulsions: Sobs clog up my choked throat and I can barely breathe, my chest heaving like a rusted iron lung. And a wounded wail pierces our ears, a traumatized twelve-year-old ambulance announcing a family emergency, an utterly unsisterly sound.

Once we calm down, Dad shows us how he's wiretapping the telephone, how he rigged up an expensive reel-to-reel tape-recorder he bought so that it comes on automatically whenever anyone picks up the receiver to make or take a call. And he swears us to total secrecy—we're not to say a word to anyone since what he's doing is illegal. Staring at our cold feet, we quietly promise to keep quiet. Then Dad brings out a four-foot-long, orange-colored cloth bag, rests one end on the floor, and loosens the string-tie. The narrow bag drops, uncovering a beautiful Marlin .22-caliber rifle, an appealing but frightful sight that shoots our words away. Dad lifts the deadly weapon out into plain view, demonstrates the clip and bolt action, and again swears us to complete secrecy. We're speechless, so it's not too hard to bow our heads and mumble yes when he calls for our commitment; no need to cross our hearts and hope to die.

After loads of bullshit and loud outbursts, mostly my father's booming voice aimed right at my mother, Mom and Dad move through their problems and restore their troubled relationship over the next several years. Or their problems eventually move through them, I should say, pushed out and passed from their bodies like a hard stool followed by a bowlful of diarrhea. Either way, they make their mess, clean themselves, flush, pull up their pants, wash their hands, and return to polite society. They remain married for some sixty-three years and die devoted and inseparable partners and parents, grandparents, and great-grandparents. My own temporarily strained relationship with my mother also eventually eases, and during my rebellious years when I'm distant from Dad, Mom keeps me from drifting out to sea as we watch old movies and sit and sip tea and talk late at night, her open ear a lifeline that holds me close to home and helps me keep my nose clean, as Dad would say.

~*~

Now that I know how the story actually ends, I know what that nightmare night with the weapon and the wailing and the wiretap didn't mean. I know now that the apparent threat to our home was hollow, the cause for concern temporary and fleeting. And fifty-four years later, I also know that that's life: irritating incidents rise up but then die down; extraordinary events loom large in the present moment and then reduce to their real size in due time, full of frightening color at first, then faded, fading away, and finally almost entirely forgotten.

These days I shake my head and roll my eyes when I consider how often and how much our lives are shaped and colored by events we don't actually experience or even witness. Too often we act on anecdotes, responding to stories we hear about what happened, even when we aren't sure how well they depict what really went on. What I heard that horrifying night certainly had a profound and lasting effect on my mind and my emotions— more profound and lasting than warranted now that I know the outcome, now that I see the bigger picture, now that I have seen the final scene and read the complete list of credits. What a great gift, this ability to alter our version of events, not in order to lie or distort, or to misrepresent facts, but to reinterpret their significance, to change how we see what happened. We thus transform the very nature of an incident or at least modify how it affects us, freeing ourselves from insidious influences. When we're fortunate, the prickly points of our emotions soften after enough time goes by, especially when we choose to perceive the past clearly—with compassion and a kindly sense of humor, one corrective lens aiding each defective eye.

~*~

Not long after that nightmare montage that mixed together the Twilight Zone, The Edge of Night, and Have Gun—Will Travel, I receive a reel-to-reel tape-recorder for my birthday. Mom and Dad endure the occasional annoyance and tolerate my amateur eavesdropping when I leave the microphone on to capture random bits of conversation; perhaps they're relieved I'm not tapping telephone calls. But tolerance becomes typical for the folks, who later welcome into our rather unusual family a variety of needful creatures, acting as part-time parents to a small pack of stray dogs, mostly mutts and nuts they bring home, like Jimmy Zolini, living with an ancient grandmother that warns him away from alcohol by begging, "Stay away from those beer gardens, Jimmy"; Tommy Jones, his mother in and out of the mental hospital; Mike Pappocapella, who even lives at our house for a few months, his mom and dad divorced and absent from his life, especially after his alcoholic father leaves for Alaska; and Joe Mubarek, his parents truly good people, but too old to relate well to him, his father as old as my grandfather.

And then there's Sally, trouble from a troubled family, an official foster child intended as a female friend for Donna; but they bang heads over boys and sparks fly, two sixteen-year-old girls going at one another's throats every time we turn around. When this doesn't work out, the foster care system begs the folks to take a brand-new baby, warning them not to become too attached. And then when Mom and Dad want to adopt little Jimmy six months later, the social workers turn them down flat because they're far too old at forty for official consideration. Brokenhearted, Mom crying, Dad trying anything that might make them both feel better, they shadow the social worker to the baby's new home, just to see where he's going, but they lose sight of the car along the way and their desperate effort ends in disappointment. Then they get another chance thirty-three years later when they decide to devote their last decade on earth to raising their great-granddaughter from ages nine months to ten years, Dad finally letting go of life once he's sure that someone else will take Kyli to school and to all her afterschool activities.

Voodoo Juju

My parents always provide the presents in our family, partly because we're still young and also because we don't receive any allowance. But I'm still sorry I don't have a gift to give my older sister for her thirteenth birthday, embarrassed that I haven't done anything on my own and afraid my family will see how selfish I am. It's too late to go to the store, and I don't have any money anyway, so I search through my things, looking for some precious possession my sister might like and I would be willing to give away. But there aren't any good choices. If I give Donna my Duncan yo-yo, she'll think I'm a yo-yo; her head will spin if I give her my top; and she'll know I've lost my marbles if I give her a handful of cat's eyes and a shooter. There's my smooth round white stone. But that would be like a little-kid gift, nice but just something I found on the ground, a stray object I find fascinating and keep in my pants pocket.

I decide that I need to make an actual gift for a girl, so I head downstairs to Dad's little shop area in the unfinished part of the basement. What can I create with limited tools and materials and my nonexistent skills, I wonder? Rummaging through wood scraps, I stir up some sawdust and one decent idea. Out of other options, I sense the occasion calls for a sacrifice that cuts to the quick: not burning a bull's entire body, not even offering his whole head—but giving up my bull's horn, a most cherished keepsake from a daylong outing I enjoyed a few years ago. A city boy in the country, I had never seen a real live bull before, so to me a bull's horn is an amazing artifact, a neat gift from my friend and fifth-grade bodyguard, Andy Brubaker, whose family raises prize-winning bulls on a big farm owned by Bing Crosby's brother Bob.

I determine to cut off the solid black tip of the bull's horn, drill a hole through the thicker side, and string it on a leather shoelace to make a rustic necklace for my sister. An inspired impression, this simple project quickly becomes a real ordeal. The horn may no longer be over the bull's head, but I'm in over mine in a matter of minutes. I may not have bitten off more Black Angus beef than I can chew, but before I know it, I'm straining to saw off and drill through more bone than I'm able. The horn doesn't lie flat on the workbench, so it's hard to hold still with one weak hand while I work the hacksaw with the other. And the tip turns out to be as hard as rock, difficult to cut. It's a cold December and I'm in an unheated area of the basement, but I'm soon sweating bullets, as my mother says, my head hot, my face and forehead wet, my underarms moist.

I saw until I'm tired, stop, relax my grip on the horn and the hacksaw, and rest my puny, cramping hands and my scrawny, aching arms. I look for visible signs of progress, but I've hardly made a mark. I begin again and repeat the process over and over: for six seconds I labor and do all the work I'm able; on the seventh, I cease from all my labors and pray for the strength to continue. After a month of Sundays, a noticeable notch appears and gradually grows deeper—to a cavernous half-inch slit. I turn the horn over and saw from the other side, trying my hardest to bring the two uneven cuts together. After another exhausting effort, I finally have the hacked tip of the horn in my hand, a relief until I realize that now I'm in even bigger trouble.

I cut too close to the hollow part of the horn and left an unsightly indentation on the flat side of the severed tip. I need to trim off this unfinished edge. But I no longer have the horn to hold onto and must keep the detached tip still with just my flimsy fingers. Oh, how I wish I had Dad's grip. And how I wish I had what he calls common sense—that would probably have prevented this problem. After another nearly endless cycle of Sabbaths—six seconds of labor, ceasing on the seventh to rest and to hope for a merciful end to my agony—I begin to appreciate how Dad developed his muscular digits. At long last, I flex my sorely-afflicted fingers and gaze down at a thin ring of black bone lying on the workbench. Now for the easy part: drill the hole for the shoelace. I suddenly see I should have drilled the hole first—while I still had the horn to hold onto—and cut the tip off afterwards. Oh, how I wish I had Dad's common sense, but I see now how he acquired this uncommon attribute, that he learned from experience, especially from his mistakes.

Crestfallen, concerned, and desperate, I remain calm enough to remember Dad's other mantra: better safe than sorry. I put on a leather glove to protect my hand in case the drill bit slips. But the bulky glove makes it more difficult to get a good grip on the tip of the horn, turning my torture into torment. I also remember that when Dad drills through hard materials, he often makes a little pilot hole with a smaller bit and then widens the opening with a bigger bit. I don't want to break the small bit and I'm afraid I might stab myself in the hand with the broken end, but I use my common sense and follow Dad's lead.

I pick up the drill and see immediately that I'm not nearly tall enough to drill directly downward, and there's nothing to stand on, so I struggle to bore a straight hole through the tip of the horn, which suddenly seems a whole lot thicker. The drill bit slips repeatedly until I finally form a shallow dent in the hard, black bone. I work until I'm tired and then take a break to rest my weary arms and my aching hands and fingers. I repeat the routine again and again: six seconds I labor and do all the work I'm able; on the seventh, I cease from all my labors and face my fears. Will I be able to complete the project or will I ruin my precious horn and still have no gift to give my sister?

Stuck between the hard tip of a bull's horn and looking bad on Donna's birthday, I find the faith to persist. After another cycle of sorry Sabbaths, a noticeable hollow slowly forms and then gradually grows deeper—to a cavernous half-inch hole, halfway home. Filings now begin to clog the opening, and that adds yet another annoying delay, but the need to blow out the coarse black powder also means more time to rest. After taking what my mother would call a slow boat to China, I eventually reach the promised land and string the ornament on the leather shoelace, an anticlimactic moment.

~*~

Donna knows nothing about the difficulties I endured, and no, I didn't imagine the entire event. But in a strange reversal of repressed memory, I recall this unpleasant experience and yet I don't remember my sister's happy reaction or even whether she ever wore my homemade present. Fifty years later, we exchange a series of email messages that add to the reality of my crude offering but also highlight our distinct ideas about the nature of the necklace: is it a piece of junk or a unique form of folk art, a dreadful voodoo juju or an appealing decorative artifact?

"Here are two pictures of the necklace that you made me. Thought you'd like to see."

"Wow. That's even more horrible than I imagined."

"I didn't think my necklace was horrible at all and still don't. Wore it occasionally up until a few years ago and then forgot it was in the jewelry box and out of sight."

"I'm glad it suits your tastes if not necessarily mine. And I'm glad to know you wore it."

"Not so much taste as it was and is special because you made it. Also, it's unique and different, and I like different, and it does well with jeans and such."

In that hopefully distant day when Donna dies, maybe we should ask the funeral director to dress her in jeans and to hang the bull-horn pendant around her neck—and then place her loaded Smith & Wesson .357 Magnum pistol in her hand. I can just see her lying there in her open casket looking unique and different—and ready to guard the cemetery against all intruders, the way she would always protect and defend her four younger brothers and our mother and father against all enemies, foreign and domestic. Perhaps I should place in her other hand the nice gold pocket watch she gave me when I left home, a treasured gift for many years. Unlike me, Mr. More Selfish, Donna has long been famous in the family as a generous giver of gifts. Uninhibited by her unexceptional income, she spends more money than she can afford and shares more time than she can spare with one and all—especially with our aging parents and the ten-year-old great-granddaughter they cared for during the final decade of their lives, their own last bighearted gift.

Lucky Dog

My mother remains against the idea, an idea I developed after reading books about dogs, drooling over the photographs. I guess she doesn't want to admit that her nine-year-old, number-one son is growing up already. And I suppose she prefers to protect me from real responsibility until I'm older and ready to succeed. Perhaps it's because she was only six when TB took her mother at twenty-seven, and her grandmother coddled her for the next seven years, until she too died of tuberculosis. Mom freely confesses that she became a spoiled brat, that when other family members wanted to discipline her, her kindhearted Italian grandmother told them, "Ooh, leave her alone, she's an orphan, she has no mother." Dad has a different background and attitude. He first went to work when he was ten—to help his family and to earn money to buy things they couldn't afford to give him. I guess he wants to let me learn responsibility through actual experience, by making mistakes if necessary, what he calls learning the hard way. And I suppose he'd also like to give me what I want and what he never had as a working-class city boy.

I repeat my petition for several months until my parents finally come to a meeting of their different minds and bring home a mixed-collie puppy we call Lucky, after a dog we had when I was two, a dog I don't recall. I'm thrilled but subdued by Dad's charge to take care of the dog: feed him, worm him, clean up after him; remove burrs and brush him; check for ticks and apply flea powder. Mom and Dad will see about shots and tags. I'm diligent and do as I'm asked, and I like taking care of a living creature. I especially enjoy brushing Lucky's gray and white fur, the feel of the brush on his back, making his thick coat and bushy tail smooth and shiny.

Guided by dog obedience books, I try to train Lucky to sit and come and stay and to relieve himself outside, but I don't really know how. Rubbing a dog's nose in his indoor accidents and hitting him with a rolled-up newspaper remain common methods, but I'm reluctant to punish; that's more Dad's style than mine. Testing Lucky's ability to obey, he also lays a morsel of steak atop the poor dog's muzzle and tells him, don't touch. When Lucky licks his lips, Dad wags his big index finger and warns, unt-uh, not yet. After a long, unlucky moment, he gives the go-ahead and Lucky gobbles up the scrap of meat. I find the whole ordeal downright mean. But maybe Dad's techniques mimic the drills he learned in basic training, after he was drafted into the Army Air Corps near the end of World War II.

I'm fond of Lucky, this bright, lively creature, and we enjoy a pleasant companionship. Together we explore the countryside, we play fetch in our big backyard, and we talk, calm and quiet. We sit silent in the sun, breathing easy as I stroke his warm-blooded body and soothe our souls: all our worries dissolve into the dark ground, our rocky resting place; our anxious minds evaporate into the open air; and our spirits expand to fill the bright blue sky, condensing into clouds ready to rain gentle on a cozy day, softening the grassy landscape. I feel fortunate. I'm a lucky dog. This is what I want and what I need, now and always: peace here on earth and harmony with heaven, solitude amid communion, the solitary company of another sentient being, some body and soul that also shares the pleasures and pains of earthly experience.

I remain responsible for Lucky. I hate to chain him up all day when I'm gone to school, but allowed to roam free he risks rabies from wild animals and abuse from bigger dogs. I pound a metal stake into the dry, rocky ground, attach a chain, and clip the other end to Lucky's collar. He whines for freedom and friendship, and while I'm away he yanks on his chain and slips his collar on occasion. Dashing through the woods, o'er the fields he goes, panting all the way; oh what fun it is to run across the neighbors' yards. Lucky remains a lucky dog for the next few years, unbitten by rabid squirrels or raccoons. But then the day comes when two vicious German Shepherds that belong to a local attorney's well-to-do family injure him in an unfair dogfight. They sink their canines into his back, tear his flesh, and leave several open sores under his fur. He's testy now and impossible to pet, snapping at family members that come too close, which Dad doesn't appreciate, especially when Lucky nips at him.

We're about to move a few miles down Myers Corners Road to open a little delicatessen next to a small country restaurant that makes tasty rotisserie chicken. Mom and Dad have rented a tiny store with a storage shed and walk-in cooler out back, along with a big two-hundred-year-old farmhouse, all on wooded land with large trees. If the business succeeds, it will increase our family income, allow my mother to work at home, and help preserve my parents' struggling marriage. The store remains open from seven in the morning until ten at night, seven days a week, including holidays. Dad continues to work fulltime on the swing shift at IBM, and Donna and I help Mom after school and also work weekends and holidays—and I have little time for

Lucky, confined now to a pen in the backyard, where dogs on the free side of the fence tease him when we're not watching.

Left to recover from his injuries and to adjust to the move entirely on his own, Lucky turns wild and begins to snap at us in earnest, trying to bite our hands and legs. I feel afraid when he growls and snarls at me, his old friend. It's sad to see Lucky lost like this, and I feel gloomy and guilty. One day he goes for Dad again, and that's the last straw for a man that feels responsible to protect his family from this now crazed animal. I come home from school and Mom tells me Dad decided we couldn't keep Lucky any longer and he had to take him to the pound. There's little hope they'll find him a new home and he'll probably be put to sleep. I'm sad and subdued, and angry, with Dad and with myself. I understand Dad's decision, but I also feel left out, like I didn't even have a chance to defend my poor dog. But there's nothing to be done now, nothing at all; it's all already said and done—done but not buried.

I guess Lucky and I grew up together during the too few years of our fleeting friendship. We began as a boy and a puppy and we end as a young man and a dead adult dog; the dog dead and gone, the young man living with the loss of a loved one, the first in a long line of losses: lost lives and loves; lost people and places; lost hopes and health; lost memories and mementos; and lost laughter, bright smiles wiped away, dissolved into tears.

Not too long after Lucky's demise, Dad buys two female pups from one of our customers, hoping to make me feel better about losing Lucky. Queenie and Princess are half-terrier and half-dachshund, with a sharp-looking black-and-brown coat and floppy hound-dog ears. They're nice to have around and it's pleasant to pet their slick, shorthaired coats and to fondle their smooth, oily ears, but they're not like Lucky. And they're even less lucky. Just when we begin to form a more affectionate friendship, they're both hit and killed by cars zooming down Myers Corners Road, just two weeks apart, come and gone in a matter of months.

It's no one's fault really, that's why they call it an accident, and puppies do wander off and end up where they don't belong. I don't blame myself, but I wonder what I might have done differently, if I could have prevented this loss. Dad doesn't say anything, but I see he feels sorry for me. At least poor Queenie and Princess are lucky enough to receive a proper burial, my first contact with corpses, except two pet turtles that died while we still lived in our apartment in Paterson. Dad and I dig holes in the soft dirt and bury the puppy bodies in the yard between the Wagon Wheel Delicatessen and the old farmhouse. I'm not frightened or upset, only aware of an awesome absence and of a palpable living presence. I remain reverent and more conscious of the great unknown, of a more expansive existence beyond my temporary little life on this tiny island in the sky, circling the sun, again and again, year in and year out.

Looking forward from the future, I also feel fortunate. I'm a lucky dog. This is not at all what I wanted but what I need, now and always: the hard but heavenly lessons of life here on earth, growing more mature, becoming wiser than before. But I still feel lonely. When will I find a friend that holds fast and lasts, forever even? When will I share the solitary company of a congenial companion, some suitable being, bone of my bones, flesh of my flesh? When will I delight in another sensitive soul, some one that also knows sorrow and joy, love and loss, some other lucky dog?

Solar System

"My very eager mother just served us nine prunes" serves as our seventh-grade mnemonic for the nine planets in our local solar system: Mercury, Venus, Earth, Mars, Jupiter, Saturn, Uranus, Neptune, and Pluto, all named after ancient Roman and Greek gods; except Earth, of course; and Pluto, demoted decades later to a dwarf planet because its name came from a Disney cartoon character, a misguided publicity stunt unappreciated by serious scientists. This alarming alteration alerts the wary and worried citizens of the solar system that even self-evident truths aren't always obvious to high-handed autocrats, that a non-heavenly governing body may decide that all planets are not created equal after all.

Unfortunately, our teacher's handy mnemonic fails to help me remember the order of our nine planets, partly because my very farsighted mother never serves nine prunes but divines the future disappearance of Pluto from the planetary pantheon and foresees the eventual renaming of Earth as Farth. The resulting new mnemonic—"My very farsighted mother just served us nine…"—ends with an as yet unknown and unnamed entity, foreshadowing the new and improved future of our native solar system. Maybe Mom will light a fire under the tiny planet Pluto: "What d'ya need a kick in the pants? Are your hands painted on or what? Don't just sit there like a bump on a log." And perhaps Pluto will get up and go to work, clear its orbit of debris, and regain its more prestigious position as a full-fledged planet.

More likely, one of Neptune's larger satellites will break free from totalitarian rule and find its happy place among the so-called civilized planets that pursue life, liberty, and their own orbit around the sun. Fully backed by the greedy interplanetary investors and profiteering corporations that finance and control worldly governments everywhere, the new ninth—Prosperus—will become a full-blown planet, plump as a plum ripe for the picking, the ultimate destiny of every sphere in our solar system. A more patriotic mnemonic will celebrate the triumph: "My violent fatherland majestically justifies sacrificing undeniably nice properties": Mercury, Venus, Farth, Mars, Jupiter, Saturn, Uranus, Neptune, and Prosperus.

Despite my inability to readily recite the names of the nine planets in their proper order, my first American success story includes this claim to fame: Richie Weston and I win second place in the Duchess County science fair for our motorized scale model of the solar system. A friend from sixth grade, Richie remains studious and well-behaved at Wappingers Junior High, a fitting counterpart to my more leisurely approach to the dull routines of academic life, our award-winning undertaking a notable exception. In this case, I recognize the importance of being earnest, making me several school years ahead of my time.

Laboring as if our lofty task is at least related to rocket science, I devote an astronomical number of hours to our plum project. I wrestle with infinitesimal fractions long on zeros, fill my spiral notebook with failed attempts, and wear out my weary eraser with far, far, far too many mistakes. I recalculate the scale sizes of the sun and the planets and their orbits over and over until I finally arrive at numbers that will work. Then I deliver the results to good old Richie. Our plan is to build the model at his house, where we have access to ample materials and a fully outfitted workshop. But when I call to ask when I should come over, Richie informs me that he and his college-educated, IBM-engineer father—who isn't always away working two jobs just to support his family—went ahead without me and completed the project on their own.

I'm knocked totally out of orbit and grounded by gravity; and dumbfounded to learn that I was left out mainly as a matter of convenience. Dazed and confused, I can barely breathe, my chest tight, my head heavy, as if my oxygen mask has failed. Richie says he's sorry, of course, in his middle-class manner, but I still feel deflated, the wind knocked out of my sails, as my mother would say, employing an earthly marine metaphor that predates the space age.

A few days later, I drag my still heavy heart and body to the science fair, where Richie and I field questions from the judges and from curious visitors concerned about the space race with the Russians. I know more about how we managed to make the model to scale and he knows more about its actual construction, of course. We work together well enough to place second in our category, but a heavy, dense cloud of interpersonal dust darkens our triumph, and I don't feel elated with our win. I'm weighed down by the pretense that this is a joint accomplishment, by the knowledge that I didn't help make the model.

Richie and I each receive our own beautiful shield-shaped dark-walnut plaque, adorned with a tiny 14-carat gold medal; the official citation declares our achievement in bold black letters on a brushed aluminum background. I'm proud of our win and our award, and I treasure the plaque, but I'm still bothered by the way that I was treated. I'm left with lingering doubts, with a growing sense that nice guys get used if they aren't careful or if they fail to defend their rights. I'm still only eleven, I'm having a hard time adjusting to junior high school, and my parents still aren't getting along lately. I feel insecure and unstable, anxious and angry, and sensitive to events and comments that might diminish my dignity or reduce my value. To help protect my tender emotions, I experiment with different versions of a more outgoing public personality—class-clown, loudmouth, jerk— good preparation if I pursue a future in politics.

One day, the jerk goes berserk on Richie. I wrestle him to the cold, hard hallway floor in front of our lockers, knocking off his eyeglasses as we fall. He's more of an egghead than a superhero, and I've read every issue of Spiderman, Daredevil, and Captain America. I have him in a tight headlock before he knows what hit him. With his thick eyeglasses in danger of being broken, Richie says, "All right, that's enough." But it's not a satisfying surrender. His exasperated adult tone mimics a reprimand to an immature child, and his face reflects displeasure and disgust. I feel more like a dumb kid than a big, bad man, and I feel foolish for fighting Richie. I say I'm sorry and we return to the overcast days of our fading friendship.

Later that year, I humiliate myself again one warm day when a group of us are outside Wappingers Junior High School eating our lunch on the grass, the class-clown entertaining the troops with loud, manly language suitable for the nation's elite fighting forces: an impressive array of words for fecal matter, illegitimate children, the male offspring of female dogs, and very hot places where the wicked are punished for profanity. All of a sudden, someone grabs me by the back of the neck. Without bothering to look up or to notice the terrified faces of my rapt audience, I warn "whoever the hell that is to get his damn hands off me." When whoever the hell has hold of me fails to release his grip, I turn my head, ready to knock his damn hand away—and it's that bastard, Mr. Schitzen, the damn son of a bitch that coaches the track teams and teaches all our physical education classes. I divert my eyes, bow my head, and shut my loud mouth.

Hauling me to my feet by the back of my neck, Mr. Schitzen orders me to police the area, to pick up any trash I find and put it in the garbage can. He either doesn't see the crutches lying on the ground nearby, he doesn't know they're mine, he's too cruel to care, or he's evil enough to see an opportunity to inflict pain. I'm certainly in no position to tell Mr. Schitzen that I'm unable to comply, that a few days before I stepped on a long nail in the tiny workshop in the unfinished area of our basement and it punctured the rubber sole of my sneaker, piercing dead center deep into the arch of my right foot, that the doctor insisted on probing the wound without any anesthesia, inserting a sharp instrument to ensure no rubber remained inside; so I simply do as Mr. Schitzen demands, hanging my head and dragging my hurt foot behind me, my performance instantly transformed from trumped-up comedy into an authentic tragedy. But this woeful scene isn't seen by any of the members of my disturbed audience—they're all looking down at their lunches, diverting their eyes to avoid getting caught up in my punishment.

We've all heard the true rumor about the truly villainous Mr. Schitzen and know what makes him a tough customer in class and a mean man on campus: a career-ending injury knocked him out of the Olympics, crushing his hope of earning a gold medal for America and thus becoming a bright star in our national solar system. High-octane oxygen rushed in to fill his deflated and now insecure ego with the foul air of superiority. Correctly depicting this type of high-and-mighty personality, my very earthy mother just speaks unflattering, nervy pith when she says: "He thinks his shit don't stink."

Wagon Wheel

I'm the fastest gun in Duchess County—no brag, just fact—lightening quick on the draw; and that's not easy with a long-barreled Colt .45, the gun that won the west. I sling my genuine-leather holster low on my right hip and tie it to my thigh with a leather thong, the ivory handle butt-forward like old Wild Bill Hickok. I cross-draw with my left hand and point and shoot in one easy motion, as deadly as Marshall Matt Dillon protecting the citizens of Dodge City from desperados. But ever since we moved into the two-hundred-year-old house next to the Wagon Wheel Delicatessen, with its two antique wagon wheels out front, I feel awkward and out-of-place in the little-kid world of make-believe, much too old now to play imaginary games with my three younger brothers, although I still join in on occasion to help them out and for something to do.

One day we're down in the new housing development under construction in a nearby neighborhood, acting out a childish combination of cops and robbers with Western six-guns. We're pretending the robbers hid their loot inside a cinder block, on top of a tall stack of loose blocks, supplies for the foundation wall on a new house. I have my long-barreled Colt .45 in my left hand, drawn and ready, on the lookout for the thieves in case they return to their hideout during our search. And here they come. I hurry, hoping to retrieve the stolen diamonds before the robbers arrive. Reaching up with my free hand, I trip over a cinder block lying on the ground and fly headlong toward the stack of blocks before me. The long metal barrel hits the blocks at an angle and spins around as I fall forward. Unable to catch my balance, I ram the gun barrel through my top two front teeth and plunge to the ground. I'm stunned. A surge of pain numbs my mind as my hand moves to cover and comfort my mouth. Game over. Time to return to reality. Time to grow up.

I stumble back over to the store to show Mom and Dad the damage, about to spread beyond my broken teeth into their uninsured pocketbook. Dad makes a close amateur inspection with a flashlight. The bottom half of one front tooth broke off and left a long, crooked edge. The other tooth is sheared in half at a sharp angle, the nerve completely exposed, the broken fragment rammed into the ridge behind my teeth. It only hurts when I breathe, as they say, when I open my mouth and let the air in, when I try to eat or smile or laugh. Fortunately, this isn't a laughing matter, unless you have a sick sense of humor. But this is only the beginning; wait until the dentist puts his hand to the plow and his shoulder to the wheel. During a long series of painful appointments, he pokes needles into the roof of my mouth, just behind my front teeth; extracts the stray fragments; performs a root canal; and then grinds down the broken teeth, leaving two stubs covered with caps he plans to replace with porcelain-covered gold crowns, but not until I turn eighteen, six long years away. No smiling at pretty girls now—and I was just beginning to notice their appealing appearance.

I withdraw further inside my shy, quiet cocoon, reading my Marvel comic books, rearranging my large collection of baseball cards, and walking in the woods and fields that surround our house. And I lift weights alone in my room so I won't be a weakling and have sand kicked in my face by a bully at the beach like that loser in the ad for the Charles Atlas bodybuilding program. But I'm also growing up in ways I hadn't anticipated, laboring at the Wagon Wheel Delicatessen, learning to work and handle real responsibilities. I haul cases of canned and bottled beer and soda from the walk-in cooler in our distant outbuilding all the way down to the store, which sits right on Myers Corners Road, testing my increasing strength and endurance. Moving quickly so I don't freeze to death, I pile the heavy cases onto a hand truck and then I drag the load over rough ground, bottles rattling to beat the band, trip after trip after trip. I carry the cases inside and stock the refrigerators with Pepsi, Coke, Cott, Costa, and 7-Up; and with Pabst, Schaefer, Rheingold, Ruppert, and Miller High Life, the champagne of bottled beers.

Coming out from my little cocoon, I also wait on customers, following Dad's detailed instructions, careful to show respect and always express appreciation. I greet people when they come in and ask how I can help. I slice their lunchmeat, careful not to cut off my fingers. I weigh each kind of cold cut on the scale and wrap the order in waxed paper. I scoop Mom and Dad's homemade potato and macaroni salads into containers. I write the prices on each item as I go and then punch the numbers into the old-fashioned cash register. I hit the total button, grasp the wooden handle, and pull down the big metal arm to open the drawer. Ring. Ring. I place the customer's bills in plain sight on the little ledge above the drawer and slowly count the change into their outstretched hand. I say please and thank you at every turn, and have a good day.

Working at the deli, Donna and I get an eyeful and an earful of totally unfamiliar adult behavior. We watch men pick up a couple of quarts or six-packs of beer on their way home from work every night. We hear how their wily wives buy our Mom's homemade spaghetti and meatballs and eggplant parmesan and tell their husbands they made it themselves. We also hear how some husbands hit their wives and children and that there's a wife-swap group down in the new housing development. When the occasional oddball customer comes in, I lie on the cold floor behind the refrigerated display cases and choke down laughs while Donna deals with their weird quirks. After a while, we're able to run the deli almost entirely on our own—we even sell cigarettes and also beer—allowing my parents to take a brief vacation, spend time together, and warm up their tepid and argumentative marriage. Grandpa Ross owned a neighborhood grocery back when he was a young married man, so he comes up from New Jersey to watch us work while Mom and Dad are away for a week.

In addition to my regular duties at the deli, I help Dad pick out candy at the wholesaler in Poughkeepsie when we need to replenish our inventory. For some reason, he thinks that I know what's happening at the candy counter, that I have a real feel for what sells, but I don't know what our customers want, I only know what I'm eating. I wish we could act like two kids in a big candy store, but instead we play our parts as dispassionate adult entrepreneurs, concerned with sales and profits, not our own sweet tooth. Dad's taste for sweets lasts for a lifetime: Eighty-three, sporting dentures, and dying of lung disease nearly half a century later, he makes what turns out to be his last request when he asks my brother Hank for a Hershey's chocolate bar from the hospital vending machine. But Dad breathes his final breath moments after my brother returns—before he finishes his favorite candy bar, which he decided didn't appeal after all once he took a few nibbles.

Back at the Wagon Wheel, I inhale enough sweet treats to choke a horse, as my mother would say. I can't bite with the temporary caps that cover my broken front teeth, but I'm still able to ingest every sugary snack in sight, all free at our family store, the bill due at the dentist. There they drill and fill the huge cavities I acquire at the candy counter and off the shelves and out of the refrigerators. I don't know what drives these constant snack attacks—maybe I sense a need to supplement my daily breakfast of champions: Cocoa Puffs, Cocoa Krispies, Frosted Flakes, Fruit Loops, Lucky Charms. Or my after-school snacks: packages of Pecan Sandies, Lorna Doones, Graham Crackers, or vanilla wafers, washed down with cups of cold milk, each one enriched with several heaping teaspoons of nutritious Nestle's Quick. Hypnotized by their catchy commercial, I just can't stop with only the recommended two teaspoons: "N-E-S-T-L-E-S, Nestle's Makes the Very Best—CHO—OC'LATE."

Whatever the reason, I scarf treats like I have a hollow leg, as my mother would say. I chomp more Milkshakes and Baby Ruth's than Babe Ruth can shake a bat at, more Milky Ways than stars in the Milky Way, more Three Musketeers than the entire male population of France. I bite enough rigid Bit O' Honey bars and hard Necco wafers to crack the Jolly Green Giant's giant teeth. I masticate millions of Milk Duds and Twizzlers and Chuckles and Switzer's licorice chunks. I munch Smarty's and M & M's and chomp Chunky's and Nestle's Crunch bars and Reese's Peanut Butter Cups. I devour boxes of Scooter Pies and Tastykake Krimpets, my favorite. I demolish cases of Drake's Coffee Cakes and Ring Dings and Devil Dogs and Yodels. I gobble a host of Hostess cupcakes and fruit pies and Twinkies and Ding Dongs and Sno Balls. I stuff my mouth with Cracker Jacks: "Popcorn, candy, peanuts, and a prize, that's what you get inside—Cracker Jacks." I chew thousands of sticks of Juicy Fruit gum. And I guzzle enough bottles of soda and Yoo-hoo to fill up an Olympic-sized swimming pool, swishing drinks like they're coming out my ears, as my mother would say.

For some reason, the Wagon Wheel Deli isn't earning a good profit, even though Donna and I work for free or for a small informal allowance. Well, I suppose our pay actually consists of nominal cash rewards and all we can eat. Donna's also snacking at the store big time, along with our three younger brothers. But most of the profits go to our two new dentists anyway, fresh out of dental school in time to found their practice on the first family of tooth decay; plus, now we're nourishing the whole neighborhood with this latest all-American diet.

Perhaps the Wagon Wheel also isn't making much money because Dad shoots from the hip when it comes to calculating the food costs. After all, he learned to cook in the Army Air Corps, and calculating costs isn't their strong suit; shooting from the hip, however, is highly valued, along with flying by the seat of your pants. I guess he's guilty of operating a deli under the influence of military recipes, in which pancake batter, for instance, is made with flour measured by the pound and eggs by the dozen. Generous and fair, Dad's also committed to two contradictory practices: he isn't about to overcharge anybody— not even for Mom's succulent Italian meatballs or her famous eggplant parmesan—and he's determined to "put some meat on that sandwich." To make a hero, Dad splits a whole loaf of Italian bread, lays on a pound of salami and prosciuttini and capicola, plus plenty of provolone, a whole sliced tomato, and loads of lettuce. And then he only charges a few bucks for the whole big shebang. No wonder crowds of construction workers flock in for lunch.

The Rifleman

Despite my deadly diet, I'm growing up but not out, and I'm still having a hard time holding up my pants, even after Dad punches extra holes in my belt with an ice pick. My waistband scrunched up several inches, I'm definitely not too big for my britches. But I'm responsible enough now to go from a boy's toy to a young man's weapon, from a realistic replica to a real gun. I'm ready to hang up my Colt .45 and shoulder the pump-action, spring-air Daisy BB gun I get for my twelfth birthday, plus plenty of ammunition and paper targets. It's a classic rifle, with steel construction, a removable screw-in 50-shot tube, and an adjustable rear sight. Mom worries that I'll hurt myself or hit someone. Dad looks me in the eye and gives me the lowdown: "Be careful. Keep the gun aimed at the ground when you're not shooting. Make sure others are behind you before you fire. And never point a gun at anyone."

I spend all my spare time practicing until the day grows dark, and I quickly become a lethal shot, rivaling the Rifleman, my favorite television hero, a man who defends his family from outlaws and his community from unscrupulous characters. But I become an unscrupulous character myself when I decide Dad means never point a gun at another human being, but that it's okay to shoot at innocent animals. Fortunately, it's easier to hit tin cans or paper targets nailed to the trunk of an oak tree than to kill a flesh-and-blood bird perched amid high branches. A would-be all-American boy, I try, try, and try again until the sobering day I finally succeed. I raise my rifle, aim, fire, and an anonymous bird gets it in the neck. A darkening red spot appears strangely artificial against its fine gray feathers, like a scarlet stain applied to a museum display to make an inanimate stuffed animal look alive.

We share an everlasting moment of suspended animation while the poor hit bird poses for a still-life portrait or an old-fashioned photograph. And then—in an illuminating flash—it lets loose and tumbles through the chill evening air. Falling from high overhead, the inert body ricochets from branch to branch until it lands lifeless in the bushes below, rustling the dry, brown leaves. Crash. Crack. Thump. Silence. I'm sad and sorry, guilty, and afraid. I approach, cautious and concerned. I bow down and gaze at the lone, dead bird lying on the chill, barren ground, its final resting place. And I leave, alone, my hands and nose cold, the gray sky now dim as the sun sinks into the earth, the heavenly light buried beneath its terrestrial blanket for another night.

I never again shoot a bird just to watch it die, and today I live among the fowls of the air in delightful variety, the fascinating company of the winged-ones. Some fifty years later, I enjoy the congenial companionship of blue jays, wrens, robins, and ring-necked pheasants; quail, flickers, and the occasional hawk; and the dear mourning doves, coo-cooing the summer sun asleep and who-who-who-ing me awake early in the morning: time to rise and shine, as my mother would say, the sun alive again, his face glorious above the mountains behind my house.

But back at the Wagon Wheel I've yet to learn a much harder lesson—never shoot yourself in the foot, especially on purpose and at close range. I miss a target one day and hit my corduroy coat lying nearby and notice the BB doesn't penetrate the cloth. I deduce that my rifle's not powerful enough to pierce this type of material; after all, this is only a youth rifle recommended for ages ten and older with adult supervision, not a CO_2 pellet gun made for hunting small animals. Armed and overconfident, I'm ready to demonstrate my newfound knowledge.

Suffering increasing financial trouble, my parents borrow money from a loan shark that lives in New York City—courtesy of a referral from our new neighbor, Faye Narcocicio—and her relative invites us all to spend the weekend at his country house in the Catskills. Late one sunny afternoon, my brothers and I are out walking in the hills with Bobby and Porky Narcocicio and their cousins, two cruel teenage girls who've been teasing and tempting me all morning. I'm toting my Daisy BB gun, of course, and everyone's crowing about killing a squirrel, and I calmly declare this rifle's not even powerful enough to penetrate a heavy piece of cloth. And they don't believe me. And I get to running my mouth about how it won't pierce the thick rubber that covers the toe of my red canvas Keds. They're all shaking their heads, and I decide I should go ahead and prove my point.

I remember Dad's reminder to be careful, but I'm sure it's safe. Besides, Dad says keep the gun aimed at the ground when not shooting, make sure others are behind me before firing, and never point a gun at anyone. He doesn't say don't place the barrel against the toe of your sneaker and fire at your own foot. But he also never told me not to ram a gun barrel through my front teeth. Then again, Dad always tells us to use our common sense, which may also mean listening to the common voice, and everyone's yelling for me not to try it, no, don't, don't do it. And I'm telling them it's okay, calming them all down for the grand finale. I'm so cocksure of myself, I won't be deterred, like American politicians who insist they're right and everyone else is wrong. I refuse to recognize I don't have common consent for my proposed course of action and that it isn't wise to act without public support.

I calmly and carefully rest the rifle against the rubber toe of my all-American sneaker. It's so quiet you can hear the air, the crowd holding its collective breath. Ready... No need to aim... Hesitate... Inhale... Squeeeze the trigger... Bam! It turns out I was right and the BB doesn't pierce the surface. But it drives the rubber directly into my ring toe with enough force to spark the most amazing pain. It's like I'm at a local Carnival: "Step right up. Test your strength." I swing the big mallet, aiming to hit the strength tester hard enough to send the puck racing up the tower to ring the bell. But I hit my own toe instead and the pain runs up my body and rings my brain, traveling from my foot to my face with a loud emergency message: "Surprise, Mr. Big Mouth. You're an idiot, not an expert, Mr. Hot Shot." Big time embarrassed, I hide my immense discomfort and play down my pain, saying I'm okay, that I'm hardly hurt at all. I try to walk without letting on how tender the toe feels, but I move like a city boy in a barnyard, wearing his Sunday shoes.

As we head back to the house, I whisper to keep quiet about what happened because I don't want my parents to take away my beloved BB gun. I've punished myself enough already, and I've already learned a good lesson, a lesson I later see goes well beyond guns—never shoot yourself in the foot, a lesson yet to be learned by far too many of our career politicians and corporate moguls.

Other lessons are yet to become clear. Later that week, we're still staying at the loan shark's country house in the Catskills, and Dad lets me take his Marlin .22 rifle, with mounted scope, out into the hills. I make sure everyone's behind me and lead the way like I'm the pied piper, pointing the gun at the ground, safety on. We soon spot an innocent groundhog off in the distance, sitting upright outside his hole. There's no question about being able to kill an animal with this weapon, which I wisely choose not to test against my fearless left foot. Already sorry about shooting a little bird with a BB gun, I'm apparently unable to dispatch a mammal with a real rifle. I empty a seven-shot clip, bullets blasting the dirt at his feet and on either side while the groundhog watches the show, mocking my inadequate aim as I move closer for each attempt. I'm definitely a better shot when facing down paper targets and tin cans, yet another reason to be against going to Vietnam in a few years—to fire a deadly weapon at other human beings while they blast me to kingdom come.

~*~

To protect ourselves and our property from the so-called bad guys, both real and imaginary, Dad places a loaded .38 caliber semiautomatic pistol under the counter at the Wagon Wheel Delicatessen. Donna and I aren't allowed to touch it, and thank God we never need it. After we close the store and move back to our house up on the other end of Myers Corners Road, the handgun serves a more congenial purpose. On New Year's Eve, Dad carries the pistol out to the front porch, safety on, pointing the gun carefully toward the floor as the family follows. He makes sure that everyone's behind him. And then he aims high above the dark woods across the road and fires a few friendly rounds, announcing another fresh start and better days ahead.

Champions

One sunny summer afternoon, Mr. Madigrosso, a big bully of a man, marches into our yard, with Richie and Bobby in tow, determined to defend his family honor, fussing and fuming and insisting that I fight his son. He doesn't even ask to speak to our mother, he just starts spouting off about settling an offense against his son, or both his sons, his entire family, the whole human race. His ranting and raving is hard to follow, but I gather he's up in arms about a remark I made during a softball game in our backyard, much ado about nothing. He wants a battle between chosen champions. Richie and I will fight bare-fisted, not to the death—we're still five and six years too young to put our lives on the line for family, God, and the federal government—just far enough to satisfy Mr. Angry Neighbor's twisted sense of justice.

Mom has an ear for trouble, and when she hears a loud, unfamiliar, and angry voice, she comes out onto the back porch to see what's going on. If Richie's mother ever came out of her house, we might have a counting out rhyme played out in person: My mother and your mother were hanging out clothes. My mother gave your mother a punch in the nose. What color was the blood? In a much less contentious mood, Mom tries to convince Mr. Madigrosso to forget this crazy nonsense and take his kids and go home, for crying out loud, but he isn't budging. Richie's secretly rooting for my mother to win the argument, his eyes wide, his face pale and afraid. He knows that I'll box his ears, as my mother would say. The two of us together don't weigh nearly as much as one heavyweight, but I'm stronger and longer than Richie, slightly bigger and certainly more muscular. And he's seen me blast a softball out of our yard and into far-right field, an empty lot between our houses filled with waist-high grass.

After wasting her time and her breath, Mom finally gives up, exhaling and shaking her head, disgusted with Mr. Madigrosso's stubborn stupidity. I swear I hear her mutter "stupid ass" under her breath, just loud enough to let Mr. Angry Neighbor know what she really thinks of him and his primitive parenting. Mr. Madigrosso wins the battle, but Richie loses the war. It's all over in a matter of minutes, before he knows what hit him, as the saying goes, although in this case he does know what hit him.

We put up our dukes and circle around each other, clumsy and hesitant. Hoping to make a good showing in front of his father and everyone else, Richie takes a few awkward swings, but he never lays a glove on me, and not just because we aren't wearing boxing gloves. I'm not faster than greased lightning, but I know how to move my feet and stay out of his way. I never lay a glove on Richie either, but my bare fists punch him in the face more times than I really want to, his battered nose and lips bleeding, his cheekbones all bruised. We go at it until he's had enough, or until his father thinks he's had enough, or until my mother finally convinces his father that he's had enough, that he's only going to get more of the same, that this is ridiculous, outrageous, pitiful, for God's sake.

61

We give Richie credit for fighting even when he didn't have a chance, but mostly we feel sorry for him—sorry his father is a jerk and sorry he'll give Richie a hard time when they get home. "You do what you have to do," my Dad would always say, and Richie did what he had to do, take a pounding in front of his father and his friends. I also did what I had to do, beat up a neighbor to satisfy his father's warped sense of family honor. A few weeks later, we exchange a quiet, casual apology, and then we're back to business as usual, as if that afternoon had never happened, once again playing friendly but competitive softball games that often include a cute platinum blonde with a crush on a certain heroic hitter; it's not all one-sided, but she's too young for me, and I'm too shy to say or do anything anyway, so I hold her at arm's length, a softball bat between us, careful not to crush her crush during our occasional awkward conversations.

~*~

A few years ago, my brother Hank emails me a photograph out of the blue. The message is one of his childish challenges: "Go ahead, dude, guess who that guy is. He now lives near Myrtle Beach, South Carolina. We last saw him as a teenager, but to me he looks exactly the same except for the weight. Bob and Ken didn't get it." I look the picture over carefully, but it doesn't ring any more bells for me than it does for our other two brothers. "I don't get it either," I write back, "something familiar about the front teeth, but that's about it."

But just as soon as my brother identifies the unknown figure in the photograph, I see the resemblance. There he is after all these many years, standing on the beach, his arm around his wife, the waves of the Atlantic Ocean in the background. It's definitely Richie Madigrosso, wearing dark sunglasses, a beige shirt and matching baseball cap, and a big smile—tanned, fat and happy, and none the worse for wear, as my mother would say. I don't feel any familiar flood of nostalgia, but for a faint, peaceful moment I feel like all's right with the world. I wonder whether Richie remembers that afternoon his father insisted on turning our little tiff into a full-blown battle, a passing squabble into an unforgettable fight, and I wonder how he feels about it. I also wonder why I still tell this story from time to time. Is it because I've never been at all in favor of fighting, with fists or words, and because I always feel bad afterwards—win, lose, or draw? Or is it because I learned early in life to prefer peace over warmongering and friendship over animosity?

Pythagorean Theorem

Master of areas and angles and arcs, and of squares, rectangles, triangles, and circles, my tenth-grade geometry teacher also rules over an arcane teaching technique. Rather than merely mark our presence or absence when he runs down the roll, Mr. Falcone asks if we've completed the homework assignment. And each time anyone admits neglect or failure, he repeats a disheartening ritual in behalf of the pitifully unprepared and the woefully inadequate. With a melodramatic wave of his hand, Mr. Football Coach banishes everyone who hasn't succeeded, intoning his command like he's W. C. Fields cast in an opera. "In the back of the room," he drones through the bullhorn of his bulbous nose and the corners of his thin, compressed lips, emitting a resonant, room-filling sound that echoes off the cold floor.

As the dread wheel of fate signals our unfortunate destiny, we each rise from our desk, pivot 180°, and join the lengthening lineup along the back wall of shame. Facing forward, we stand perpendicular to the floor and adjacent to the wall for the entire class period, trying to think of the strange Pythagorean theorem and the many other enigmatic rules of plane geometry. "Always, always, always think—ya gotta think," Mr. Falcone monotones, his index finger tick-tocking, a monotonous human metronome. "Always, always, always remember the Pythagorean theorem," he continues. And "never, never, never..." forget some baffling formula I no longer recall, hypnotized at the time. We dream of the day when the clouds of confusion will clear, the cherished day when we will remain in our seats and be counted among the privileged problem-solvers of our time, those foreordained to figure out how to bring a precious bag of rocks back from the moon; how to win the arms race and vaporize the planet before the Russians; how to get our head out of our butt in Vietnam; how to export our capitalist economy to every nation, tongue, and people so that everyone on earth might enjoy Coke, Pepsi, Twinkies, Salem cigarettes, and a long, healthy life.

Unfortunately for us, the wall of shame isn't the best place to see how to solve complex problems, and we all fall farther and farther behind. Truly dedicated to helping us master the material and obviously advanced for his time, the visionary Mr. Falcone holds help-sessions after school for those that have a bona fide disability—those unable to determine the areas and angles of abstract geometric figures due to a genetic defect yet to be discovered by the would-be problem-solvers of our generation. We appreciate the assistance and take full advantage of the opportunity. The partially disabled learn to do plane geometry; the totally disabled learn how to amuse an audience.

My ninth-grade algebra teacher, Mr. Mormello, claims that I don't even suffer from a disability at all, that I'm clearly capable of higher mathematics. I just need to apply myself. He tells my parents that my IQ scores are quite high and that there isn't any logical reason I shouldn't continue on in the college-prep track that requires both geometry and trigonometry, plus calculus if possible. I'm not sure that my parents have ever even heard of trigonometry or calculus, but I'm sure they know that a high IQ is better than a low IQ. After all, higher is always better than lower in America, where climbing the high ladder of success is the name of the game, and attending college is a good way to get ahead without breaking your back. But Dad also often tells us that many IBM engineers have that piece of paper but lack common sense. And he's the one whose suggestions are often accepted and rewarded by the company, much to the chagrin of his more educated superiors.

I reluctantly agree to give the college-prep track the good old college try and end up in Mr. Falcone's tenth grade geometry, where I'm frequently ushered to the back of the room despite my high IQ, which is dropping like a rock, my brain power oozing out my shoes from too many hours on my feet. If I had properly applied myself in ninth grade algebra, I could probably plot my falling IQ on a graph, or would that require calculus? Unfortunately, my diminished mental capacity leads me into bad behavior that just doesn't add up, although it might make more sense if I could confirm that I'm under the influence of a secret posthypnotic suggestion.

One afternoon I'm standing in a wavy line that departs from the X–Y-axis by an unknown number of degrees, waiting to show Mr. Falcone my sorry solutions to our geometry exercises. The ignorant kid in front of me bends over Mr. Falcone's rectangular desk and writes corrections on his paper, pretending to always, always, always think. I step behind Mr. Falcone and gaze down at his bald scalp, glistening in the bright light. I can't calculate just how many square inches are bare, but the area is bounded by a semicircle of dense hair above the ears, with two wispy tufts decorating the back of the crown, clearly the head of a football player whose hair has been worn off by his helmet. Possessed by the mesmerizing power of geometric figures, I glance up at the boys in the back of the room, slowly lower my hand crazy-close to Mr. Falcone's smooth cranium, and pretend I'm scratching his scalp. Sensing my presence, he twists his thick neck, broad shoulders, and trim trunk and glances up at a 45°

angle. I yank back my hand last split-second, like I'm saving my fingers from a deadly mousetrap that snaps without warning.

A few minutes later, I'm safely back in the back of the room, choking down chuckles with amused members of my audience, when Mr. Falcone drones a firm directive to keep quiet. And then he hums out loudly, "And Dick, don't think I didn't see you trying to scratch my head." I cringe, but I cringe whenever Mr. Falcone addresses me. He decides to call me Dick without asking, and I don't like it. Nobody else ever calls me that—because it's not my name; I'm just not a Dick. Besides, it's also an obscene word you wouldn't want as your nickname, unless you're a very unpopular American president, and that's still an election, an escalating war, and a Watergate away. Perhaps I'm sensitive to nicknames ever since my sixth-grade teacher, Mr. Paul, nicknames me Peanut because I'm much smaller than all the other boys, although only because I'm also much younger. Sadly, his affectionate but belittling pet name follows me into my humiliating first year of junior high school. I wish he had dubbed me Little Richard instead, foreshadowing my success as a famous and influential rock and roll singer.

Another day in tenth grade geometry, I print a small sign that says THINK and prop it up proudly on my desk, facing the front of the room at an acute angle whose size I'm unable to determine, an unsuccessful attempt to mock our class motto, also the official motto of IBM, the principal employer of college graduates in our area. Mr. Falcone plays it straight and endorses my efforts with great enthusiasm: "That's right, Dick, ya gotta think. Always, always, always think." And I do. After I flunk geometry, I think that if high school is this bad, why would I want to go on to college and continue the torture. That's like insisting on four more years after a failed first term as president. I eventually think yet again and retake geometry my senior year, but in the meantime, I take electronics shop, which turns out as impenetrable and uninteresting as any math class. Later I also try auto shop, but once I see it's going to be a long haul before we ever even look at a car, let alone overhaul an engine, I drop the class, wearied by tedious and repetitious explanations of the Bernoulli principle.

~*~

After graduation, I land a job on the IBM assembly line, but I'm bored to death and quit within a year to work fulltime at a business opportunity I pursue with my father, who hopes it will help me keep my nose clean. Dad often asks if I'm keeping my nose clean. And that's a truly legitimate concern given the many large noses in our family, an attribute that might have given us a unique opportunity to serve our country. Wise political leaders could have called upon us to blow student protesters away with a big simultaneous sneeze, but they prefer to keep the peace by the most violent means available and decide instead to send the National Guard to blast our best and brightest with M-16 rifles, making them ineligible for the draft. I don't understand it, but I never took bureaucratic calculus or trickydickonometry.

Seven years or so after I finally earn my high school diploma, a large private university approves my application without all the advanced math classes, and I never leave the world of so-called higher learning, where no one tries to call me Dick. I graduate magna cum laude, complete two master's degrees at the Yale Graduate School of Arts and Sciences, and then teach at my alma mater for more than twenty-seven years. I never use math in my academic work, but every once in a blue moon, as my mother would say, I think I recall the old Pythagorean theorem: $a^2 + b^2 = c^2$; the square of the hypotenuse of a right triangle is equal to the sum of the squares of the other two sides. Isn't that right, Mr. Falcone?

Borditis

Nearly every dreary hour, our tedious teacher redraws the same old inert diagrams of electronic circuits on the blackboard and lectures at length. He drones on and on about temperamental vacuum tubes, the main components in our small but bulky television sets. And he babbles about how tiny transistors have recently made portable radios possible. They also make our dull electronics shop class more exciting whenever we're granted time for a little independent lab work. While the instructor isn't watching, Barry Veriwacko, one of the more extremist members of our ring of revolutionaries, pulls handfuls of transistors out of the supply cabinet and performs his innovative experiments, attracting a small circle of interested observers. He connects the clamps from the heavy power supply to the short stiff wires that protrude from either end of an inch-long transistor. Then he amps up the electricity until the transistor bursts into bright red, white, and blue flames, glowing like a toasted marshmallow held far too close to an Independence Day campfire. But our earnest efforts to test the load capacity of transistors and to celebrate American freedom from foreign rule remain unappreciated—I suppose because our teacher doesn't welcome black burn marks on his wooden countertop.

Aflame with patriotic enthusiasm, Veriwacko persists in his courageous effort to discover exciting scientific knowledge, carrying out numerous experiments in his quest for success. I watch and admire, but I worry about all the damage to school property and the danger of serious consequences, anxious that these thrilling attempts to really push the envelope in electrical engineering might blow up in our faces—concerns not shared by a government that justifies underground nuclear explosions because they don't make visible marks on the earth's sensitive surface. Yet I still learn a lot about the load capacity and also the flammability of transistors. More important, the pyrotechnics relieve my borditis, a neurological disorder I suffer throughout high school, a condition aggravated by mind-numbing teaching techniques and tiresome course content. Lack of intellectual stimulation may lead to painful or even fatal episodes, so I need to forego classes every so often to avoid being bored to tears, bored stiff, or bored to death.

Unfortunately, I'm absent the day the power supply catches on fire and miss what witnesses claim was a truly illuminating educational experience, highly therapeutic for the worst case of borditis. I'm safe at home the remarkable morning Veriwacko figures out how to electrify several transistors simultaneously and overloads the poor expensive power supply in the process. When I return to school, the power supply is absent—and so is Veriwacko, his revolutionary experiments suspended by a totally unenlightened administration. A burned countertop and charred wall are still there; and they give proof through the night that the flame of freedom once burned brightly in that dreary place, transistors red glare, the power supply bursting in air.

A stirring story is also still gallantly streaming, a tattered flag of hope blowing in the breeze, boosting our low morale as we march back to our kingdom of boredom, to sit silently and stare blankly at the dreary blackboard. Luckily, a truly dreamy girl in biology comes to soothe my borditis and to rescue me from this reality. When I need a vivid vision to arouse my imagination, Sue's pretty, freckled face appears in my open, empty mind, her wavy red hair and musical voice raising a genuine flight of fancy. I rehearse actually asking her out until I finally find the awkward words, but I call much too close to the dreamt-of day and she's already busy for the next basketball game. Her regret sounds sincere but I'm too shy to try again, especially since she's older and more mature, or so I imagine.

~*~

I wish I had recognized the great importance of being earnest about always attending all my classes, for then I would have been present for Veriwacko's grand finale. But I had already learned from freshman wood shop the importance of not being too earnest when I earnestly undertook to make my mother a large wooden serving bowl, like the one my friend Colin made for his family. I'm so earnest in my efforts that when I finally remove the initial block of wood from the lathe, I have a small, shallow candy dish. Mom keeps it in a cabinet where it won't wear out from overuse. Two years later, my classmates and I earnestly perform *The Importance of Being Earnest* in Mr. Realie's junior English class, but I don't really get it, not even the pun on the title character's name.

I eventually learn my lesson and years later my attendance soars to near perfect in the much less rigid and more stimulating educational environments of college and especially graduate school. And as a more mature adult, I likewise learn to maintain diligent attendance at church for decades—except for a rare lapse almost thirty years ago, when I stay home one Sunday and miss an exciting event that rivals the lost day the power supply caught fire. Old Sister Boring, our longtime matronly chorister, faints while conducting a congregational hymn and falls over

71

backwards on the stand, her arms and legs sticking up in the air like an upturned turtle. Her embarrassed husband leaps from his seat on the front row, runs up the stairs to the stand, and tries his best to cover her up, bringing her gray dress back down over her exposed slip and stockings. Regaining consciousness but still confused about where she is or what her husband might be up to, she shoos him away, scolding loud enough for the entire congregation to hear her inappropriately intimate refrain, "Get off of me John, get off of me."

Cosmic Egg

With his old working-class concern for what he calls common sense, I'm sure Dad knows that what came first was neither the chicken nor the egg but a rooster and a hen. After all, Dad had a chicken and egg store with his oldest brother back when my folks were first married, before my sister and I each began our bodily life on earth as one of our mother's fertilized human eggs. I first learn how amazing chicken eggs are the day that Joe Mubarek demonstrates their impressive physical properties in the kitchen of our house on Myers Corners Road. Dad meets Joe at the Grand Union Delicatessen in Wappingers, where they both work part-time, Joe while attending Duchess Community College, Dad while working fulltime at IBM.

Joe Mubarek began his own bodily life on earth as a fertilized human egg created by his now middle-aged mother and a father now old enough to be his grandfather, both retired from the U.S. Navy. Joe's a bright, hard-working, down-to-earth, good guy, plus he's Polish, and most of Mom and Dad's friends were

Polish during their early years together. Dad likes Joe and brings him home for supper one night in the fall of 1966. With his courteous and respectful manner and his quick wit, Joe quickly becomes a favorite and close family friend, and our house soon becomes his home away from home. He often joins us for supper, coming early and leaving late. He tells us funny stories, recites Bill Cosby monologues from memory, and amuses us with his rapid-fire wisecracks. He's hilarious. We laugh until our cheeks ache and we gasp for breath.

A drummer, Joe constantly pumps his left leg and taps his fingers on the kitchen table, or he spins a butter knife or flips his matchbook, puffing cigarettes like he owns shares in the tobacco company, as my mother would say. And he entertains us with his creative physical comedy, with silly juvenile antics—like when Mom serves her homemade chocolate-chip cookies covered with powdered sugar, and Joe puts a whole cookie in his slightly open mouth and coughs, filling the air with a cloud of sweet white dust. But this isn't nearly as amazing as what happens one day when my parents happen not to be home.

One afternoon Joe announces that the common chicken egg is ingeniously designed, that if you hold it in your hand just right, it won't break no matter how hard you squeeze. We want to test his claim, of course, and he's more than willing to prove his point. Joe takes an ordinary egg in his right hand and stands over the kitchen sink, holding the egg just so, palm up so we can see what's happening. He then applies firm pressure, and sure enough, the egg doesn't break. "Squeeze harder," we taunt, egging him on.

Joe was the big star fullback on his undefeated high school football team, and his regional records for the high jump, the discus, and the shot-put remain unbroken for many years. He has massive thighs, a broad chest and beefy shoulders, and big biceps, mighty forearms, and a powerful grip. He squeezes the egg in earnest until his biceps bulge, the veins stand out on his neck, and his face turns red. "Squeeze harder, squeeze harder,

harder, harder," we yell, louder and louder, cheering him on to victory. And sure enough, the egg still doesn't break. But it shifts ever so slightly in Joe's sweaty hand, just enough to move out of the perfect position, the precise position where it won't crack under all this immense pressure. Mimicking the cosmic moment when the big bang gave birth to the known universe, the egg suddenly explodes and expands to fill the universe of our cramped kitchen. It splatters outward onto the front of Joe's shirt, splashes upward onto the outside surface of his thick eyeglasses, and soars to the ceiling above his head. With his hand palm-up to keep the egg visible, not a drop drops into the sink. We stand transfixed in the midst of a truly cosmic event. Joe looks embarrassed and we are all stunned. Holy shit.

After his dear friend Richie Miller dies, Joe spends even more time at his second home, and he and I become close friends, even though he's five years older, passing many hours in quiet conversation. Later we learn to play tennis from an old library book, spending time outdoors, and we play plenty of chess. We're brothers at heart, much deeper thinkers than the rest of the crowd that hangs out at my house. We're more intelligent, more serious and searching, more concerned with cosmic questions, with good and evil, with right and wrong, with the consequences of our actions. How did poor Richie Miller die? Driving fast and drunk down a winding country road, he runs off an embankment and flips his tiny sports car like he's tossing a coin in the air: heads, he loses, the removable roof crushed like a flattened beer can. He survives but he suffers significant brain damage and falls into a coma for a spell. He eventually recovers and returns home from the hospital—with an altered and much darker personality—and shoots himself in the head with a shotgun.

In early 1967, Joe enlists in the Air Force and goes to Texas for basic training and then to study Russian for nine months at Syracuse University in upstate New York, returning home on occasion to Wappingers Falls. First he sells his fire-engine red

75

Chevy Nova coupe to his younger brother John, who works as a mechanic in a local auto shop. John first became interested in the car when he tried to figure out what caused another cosmic flare-up late one night after Joe was out drinking beer at his favorite local bar. Feeling warm and toasty on a frozen winter night, Joe ambles out to the parking lot, where his stone-cold car awaits, a painted replica of Snoopy, World War I flying ace, glowing white on the left front fender, his scarf fluttering in the breeze. A curiously incompatible title—"The Red Baron"—appears underneath, turning the cartoon into an illogical image. Together they constitute a sign that the poor car suffers from a major multiple-personality disorder, an ominous omen that two incongruent identities, Snoopy and the Red Baron, battle for dominance under the hood, beneath conscious awareness.

Joe takes the keys to the Red Baron in the same right hand that squeezed an amazing mess out of the exploding egg and starts the car. Once again mimicking the cosmic moment when the big bang gave birth to the known universe, the 327-cubic-inch engine with its big four-barrel carburetors suddenly erupts and fills the enclosed engine compartment with fire and smoke, threatening destruction. Joe jumps out and throws up the hood to see what's happening: fire everywhere. A passerby scoops up a big handful of sand to throw onto the flames rising from the uncovered carburetors, a bad idea unless you want to overhaul the entire engine when this is all over. Joe tells him no way, are you crazy, and he whips off his woolen coat, a humble burnt offering, laying his lowly sacrifice to the powerful mechanical gods of American mass production on the flaming altar of the engine, snuffing out the awful blaze.

After learning the Russian language, Joe is posted to Ankara, Turkey, known among his associates as the armpit of the world. He later tells us that their toilet paper is peppered with big splinters—so you have to be careful you don't hurt your...hand. Before Joe leaves on his new foreign adventure, we tour upstate New York together, visiting a host of historic sites and natural wonders and imbibing the gorgeous countryside, a quiet week with few words. And Joe's younger brother marries my older sister, our two huge nephews to begin their bodily life on earth over the next several years as two of her fertilized human eggs, all part of the expanding universe.

Joe's superiors assign him to listen in on the radio chatter of Soviet pilots, the distrusted agents of an evil socialist empire, the archenemy of all human civilization, according to the U.S. Department of Paranoia. The equally suspicious leaders of the new Evil Empire likewise fear the eavesdropping American Air Force, suspect instrument of a vast capitalist military-industrial complex, the destroyer of all life on earth. In the end, the duped and exploited common people of planet earth regain their good old common sense and relearn what they already knew, that the root of all evil is the love of money—because it serves as the source of the power to pretend you are a false god, the center of your universe and the creator of your very own cosmic egg.

Don't Mess with Donna

You don't want to mess with Donna, no doubt about it. There's that dark night she hears something outside and comes upstairs to wake me, leaving the bedroom light off to avoid attracting attention. Mom and Dad are out late, so we're home alone with our three younger brothers in an isolated two-hundred-year-old farmhouse. I'm in a deep sleep, completely unconscious, dead to the world. Afraid of who or what might be lurking in the bushes or behind the big trees, Donna shakes me repeatedly, harder and harder, calling my name over and over in a loud whisper: "Rich... Rich... Rich..." I slowly recognize her faintly familiar voice, my brain and eyes still blurry. When I'm finally half-awake, I see my sister bending over me, close to my head and breathing hard. She's holding a large kitchen knife in her right hand, inches from my face, ready to defend the family against intruders. She insists I get up so we can check out the house and make sure everything's okay. I'm groggy and not too keen on the idea, but who wants to argue with a frightened fourteen-year-old girl when she's wielding a sharp weapon?

I wonder if this is why for several years I sleep with the covers over my head; why for decades I'm afraid of the dark and sleep with a nightlight on; why I'm so easily disturbed during the night and suffer from insomnia. I wonder if this is why when someone wakes me from a deep sleep, I put up my hands in karate-chop posture, yell loudly, and instinctively block my face with my forearms. I wonder if this why on occasion I wake up suddenly, sit bolt upright in bed, and swear I hear a female voice calling my name in a loud whisper.

~*~

You especially don't want to mess with Donna when it comes to her cars, particularly her first Pontiac convertible, a skyline blue Catalina with a white top and interior, purchased with money she made working as a secretary intern during her senior year of high school, in 1967. One night we're coming down Myers Corners Road, Donna driving carefully, our friend Tommy, an all-state wrestling champion and award-winning linebacker, along for the ride. It's pouring cats and dogs, as my mother would say, and it's dark as a bottle of India ink, not a street light in sight or a house anywhere around. We're not much more than a mile from our home when suddenly we see a car stalled in the middle of the intersection with All Angels Hill Road. Donna—no angel herself—slows way down and tries to go around without completely leaving her lane. But she comes a little too close and the front fender of the other car puts a long crease down the entire right side of Donna's beloved Catalina.

Donna and Tommy climb out to discuss the damage with the other driver, and before I know what's happening, Donna's out there in the pouring rain giving this middle-aged guy hell about what the hell he's doing blocking the intersection—look at what you did to my car, you son of a bitch. And the guy's yelling back at Donna and he calls her a dumb woman driver. Big mistake.

Donna's definitely not dumb, she's a good driver, and she's the 1968 version of a feisty frontier woman, the kind that doesn't take any shit from anybody, and especially not from any male chauvinist pig; and she must be thinking, "I'll knock you into the middle of next week," as my mother would say. Acting in behalf of women drivers all over America, Donna belts Mr. Bigot square on his bigmouth jaw, swinging her fist like Joltin' Joe DiMaggio swung a baseball bat back in Dad's day.

Acting in behalf of dumb male drivers all over America, Mr. Bigot raises his hand to hit Donna back, his dim-wit brain apparently damaged by her blow. Tommy doesn't just stand there with his hands in his pockets, as my mother would say. Acting in behalf of Donna—to shield her from any further trouble—and in behalf of Mr. Bigot—to shield the stupid idiot from Donna—gutsy Tommy threatens that if the guy lays one hand on her, Tommy will lay him out. (I prefer my mother's more graphic warning whenever anyone even thinks about raising a hand to her: "Don't you dare; I'll break it off and hit you with the bloody end.") Now using his hard head for more than a hat rack, as my mother would say, Mr. Bigot quickly decides against a close encounter with the solid surface of Myers Corners Road, firm evidence that there's still hope for the macho version of the American male.

But this doesn't end the argument-cum-would-be-fistfight. The next thing I know we're in this cramped room at the rickety old courthouse in Wappingers Falls, waiting for Donna and my parents to emerge. They're in there talking to the judge about an assault charge the other driver filed against my sister, mostly to save face. He isn't hurt but embarrassed big time about being jolted in the jaw by a gutsy seventeen-year-old girl, aka a dumb woman driver. Mom later tells us it turns out that my parents know the judge, and he tells them not to let on that they know him, and then he tries to lead Donna to admit to a less serious violation: Now you slapped him with an open hand, isn't that right? And then your stupid sister says: No. I punched him, I punched him with my fist.

Fortunately, the judge finally convinces Mr. Macho to drop the charges, Donna being so young and making a mistake. And his vehicle shouldn't have been in the intersection in the first place, and his actions afterwards were also incendiary.

We always laugh when we tell this family story, although it isn't so funny at the time, the trouble with the law and the damage to Donna's poor car, not to mention the damage to the other driver's diminished male ego. But we don't keep in touch, so I don't know if he buys a bigger vehicle to compensate or what he tells his wife when he comes home with his sore jaw. I also don't know what made Donna do it. Is it nature or nurture, a matter of genetic predisposition or of attitudes she acquired at an impressionable age? Maybe she inherited a tendency toward violence. Or maybe she's operating under the influence of a story that Mom tells about the time—years before we were all born—when Grandpa Ross dragged another driver out through his open car window, smashed him in the face with his massive fist, and left him lying on the ground. You never know what course of action a story might suggest or what words might be taken to mean. But you sure wouldn't want to mess with the meaning of Donna's calamitous story, because that would mean messing with Donna, and you still don't want to mess with Donna. At sixty-six, she remains a formidable force—and now she's ready for real action with her big Smith & Wesson .357 Magnum revolver. Don't worry—she knows when and how to wield it, and she's a crack shot.

Ring Finger

I need to order my high school graduation ring during my junior year. I'm only fifteen, a couple of years younger than the other kids in my class, and rather small for my age, a hundred pounds soaking wet, as my mother would say. My hands and fingers look more like I passed the last several years making model cars, flipping baseball cards, leafing through my collection of Marvel comic books, perusing science fiction novels, and reading all fourteen volumes of the Richard's Topical Encyclopedia, not digging ditches or squeezing a grip strengthener. I want to order a ring close to my actual ring size or maybe a little larger. But Mom and my older sister Donna argue that I should focus on the future, when I will surely be much bigger, like my father. They insist I order a ring the same size as his: "You can wear it with a guard until you grow into it."

I figure I will be taller and heavier than I am now, but there's no way Dad and I will ever wear the same size ring. He's five foot eleven, weighs a hundred and seventy-five pounds, and has huge hands—with fingers that are long and strong and muscular from a lifetime of labor. His hands and fingers are so big and brawny that when he would gently but firmly place his hand over mine to show me how to work a handsaw when I was young, I felt as if my bones would break, crushed against the handle. Dad's ring size is surely more a matter of nurture than nature, a product of his hard work, not of pure genetics.

They aren't exactly stubborn or totally closed-minded, but once Mom and Donna make up their minds, they aren't about to budge, two immovable mountains. "When I know I'm right, I know I'm right" is their shared mantra. No wonder they bang heads on occasion, sparks flying like two flints struck against each other. Facing futility, fate, and the immovable mountains, I shake my medium head, shrug my narrow shoulders, throw up my slender hands, and order a piece of circular jewelry as big as a Buick steering wheel. When the huge ring arrives, it fits over my thumb, as expected, so I wear it with the guard, as planned. But the thin-edged guard rubs against my ring finger, so the two immovable mountains persuade me to replace it with a massive wad of surgical tape. Now I'm uncomfortable and embarrassed to boot. I feel like I'm a petite girl sporting her football-player boyfriend's big ring. I don't stop to think that maybe all I need is a girlfriend with fat fingers to wear my ring, but chubby girls are hard to find in this more svelte version of America.

"I'm not always right, but I'm never wrong," Mom would say, an attitude she shares with Donna. But if anything is truly possible in the land of the delusional and the home of the naïve, then it's also possible that the two immovable mountains are mistaken on occasion. And after a while, I decide they're dead wrong, that I will never grow into the ring. I pull off the tape, clean the dirty, gluey ring with rubbing alcohol, and store it in my jewelry box—its home for nearly fifty years now. At a low point in the early 1990s—underemployed as adjunct faculty with two master's degrees from Yale and four young children to support—I consider selling the ring to cover my student loan payments. But once I learn how little I can actually get for the gold, I decide to keep the ring until my bigger and better future arrives, especially now that it fits on my index finger rather than my thumb, a sure sign of the growth that the two immovable mountains promised decades before.

~*~

Dad dies in 2011, only six weeks short of his eighty-fourth birthday. I hardly recognize him lying there in his casket, his face coated with brown makeup to cover the pink blotches that mark his pale cheeks. He looks like he has finally overcome his ambivalent prejudice and become a bona fide member of a darker race. His mischievous smile and his twinkling eyes are absent, so I can't tell whether he appreciates the humor or if he's annoyed. I suspect that he's laughing out loud, a cheerful grin brightening his countenance. Dad also looks an awful lot smaller, a miniature version of himself, lacking his big upper body and his powerful forearms. I'm not quite five foot nine and weigh just one hundred and fifty pounds, but I'm taller and heavier than him at last, bigger and broader than this little mannequin man. His body and his hands have shrunk to where my wedding ring would fit his thin finger and my high school graduation ring would require a guard or a wad of surgical tape. I wonder if Dad left this tiny body behind because it can no longer contain his big heart and magnanimous spirit. Now the oldest but still smallest adult male member of the family, I'm oddly aware that my size nine feet will never fill his size eleven shoes—even if our fingers finally fit the same size ring.

Bottom Rung

It's the summer of '68, the summer before my senior year, long before McDonald's would destroy casual dining in America; before our now fat population would be force-fed at fast-food outlets; before every single item on the menu would come from commercialized corn and beef from abused animals; before a hamburger would have cheese on it, a melted mess of orange-coated crud. And long before I would ever meet a milkshake that isn't an actual drink, made of whole milk and real ice cream, mixed thin enough to sip the luscious liquid through a narrow paper straw. Every weekday, my coworker Dan and I walk to the end of the block, cross the busy city street, slip into the corner drugstore, march directly to the old-fashioned grill and soda fountain, and slide into our regular round stools at the counter, eager to eat. And every single day I order an absolutely delicious hamburger and an amazing vanilla malted milkshake. Lunchtime is definitely what I always like best about working at

Perlmutter's Furniture on Main Street in Poughkeepsie, my first real job earning steady weekly wages.

I wait and I watch with hungry, almost amorous eyes, my mouth watering, my hamburger sizzling on the grill, the high-speed mixer blending my milkshake in a cold, stainless-steel cup. And everything is ready at exactly the right simultaneous moment. The cook slides my plated, piping hot hamburger under my nose. Then he quickly pours my creamy milkshake, resting the heavy soda-fountain glass at my fingertips and the still half-full steel cup within easy reach when I'm ready for a refill, setting a small paper straw and the ticket alongside for his customer's convenience. First I finish the hamburger and the soda-fountain glass full of sweet milkshake, and then I enjoy a second dose of the succulent, ice-cream-infused malted milk as a delicious dessert, a relaxing moment before returning to work. I savor each mouthful of bona fide hamburger and genuine milkshake, but I also eat steady so we'll be sure to get back to our boring job before the end of our thirty-minute lunch hour.

Dan tries his best to hustle on the way back, but he has a hitch in his get-along, as my mother would say, handicapped by a club foot and a lame leg. His drawn-up arm pawing the air with each stuttered step, he dances along the cement sidewalk in his signature one-two shuffle, slow-slow, slow-slow, slow-slow; his bald head glistening in the noonday sun, his heavy eyeglasses inching down the bridge of his sweaty nose, his defective left eye hidden behind the dense lenses. Now a middle-aged man, he's been the porter at Perlmutter's for who knows how long. I'm his fifteen-year-old helper, hired to assist for the summer and warned by the manager not to pick up Dan's lazy habits. Vacuuming, polishing, and dusting all day long, I keep my clean nose to the grindstone and my gaze fixed on the floors and the furniture, enough to cover an entire football field. But I'm still able to glance up the tall ladder of success on occasion and see how all the managers and all the salesmen and all the delivery drivers look down their upturned noses at Dan and me and our lowly labors.

But Dan's not the only one looking at the world with one blind eye. Way up on their high horses, our supposed superiors fail to see what we do down here on the bottom rung, to see inside our work, to perceive and appreciate the art in our craft. The others also fail to sense that Dan's lack of dedication and tendency toward laziness may be because he's defeated, done in by thousands of days filled with repetitive tasks and no change in sight, other than his eventual death, preceded by a woeful retirement. And talk about lazy—what do all the salesmen do most of the day but sit in overstuffed chairs in suits and ties, twiddling their thumbs while they wait for a customer to come in? And the managers may be busy in their offices, but how hard is it to shuffle papers and get up from a desk once in a while to walk to the water cooler? And the uniformed delivery drivers between calls, all standing around with their hands on their ass and their finger up their nose, as my mother would say, running their big mouths about their so-called sexual exploits.

Unfortunately, my lowly position at Perlmutter's comes with unofficial and unwelcomed perks. I'm out front one morning mopping the tile entryway that ushers customers into the store when one of the delivery guys asks me if I'd like to go with him to his girlfriend's house: she has a younger sister that balls and you could go with her while I bang the older sister, he says. I feel intense pressure, but I'm not at all comfortable with this proposition or with his animal attitude; when I'm ready, I'd rather be with a girl I know well and have genuine romantic feelings for. I mean even my friends that have sexual experience are involved with their steady girlfriends, not sleeping with total strangers. And I'm just enjoying my first French kisses with a friendly girl visiting from out of town, here to see her cousin.

Another day, one of the salesmen corners me while I'm off alone dusting and pulls a stack of cards containing photographs of nude women from his inside suit pocket. I'm intrigued but I would rather not look under these circumstances. He insists, placing the cards in my hand and telling me to take my time. Uneasy but well aware that he's higher up the totem pole than I am, I yield to his unappreciated pressure. On another occasion, he also pressures me to accept a sexual favor from him. In his superior position, he's quite unconcerned about consequences, a complaint from a lowly porter unthinkable. Feeling repulsed and threatened, I step back, unconsciously clench my fists, and turn him down flat, and again even more forcefully when he repeats his appeal. He stops harassing me, but I still try my best to avoid another encounter, moving out of the area whenever I see him heading in my direction.

A few weeks or so later, I somehow manage to mention the incident to both my parents at an opportune time. They express their concern but show little alarm, more of a matter-of-fact reaction, just, yeah, these things happen, and yeah, that's how to handle them, but don't hesitate to defend yourself if someone tries to put their hands on you; and don't worry, I sure will. Of course this means only if necessary. I mean my folks believe in live and let live and that you leave people alone if they aren't bothering you. Mom and Dad have their prejudices but also a tolerant attitude toward others, even if they're different. When we had the Wagon Wheel Deli, Dad would bring groceries to two guys that lived together in a small cottage in the woods, explaining when I asked that some people are just that way is all, shrugging his shoulders to show he didn't get it but what does it matter to him how they live.

I'm fending for myself on Perlmutter's bottom rung as an aftereffect of Mom and Dad's participation in the installment plan, the roaring American highway to pretended prosperity: go ahead and buy now—and keep up with the Joneses—and pay later—if you can keep up with the big payments. They bought furniture on time and now they're having a hard time coming up with the money every month, so one of Perlmutter's owners hires me to supplement what they earn working three jobs. And that's why Mr. Stern asks me if I'm giving my paycheck to my parents, picking the lint off my shirt while I look at my shoes and mumble an evasive answer. He doesn't know that my folks haven't the heart to take all of the sixty-six dollars I make for forty hours work at minimum wage, that they only ask for just twenty. And that leaves me enough money to learn the new-fashioned way to get what you want, to buy my friend Jimmy's car after he enlists in the Marines and pay it off later. Sadly, the bottom rung of the ladder of success has sunk since '68. Today it would take two to three times as many weeks working fulltime at minimum wage to pay for a four-year-old Chevy Impala.

~*~

Nearly half a century has passed since my summer on the bottom rung, dusting and vacuuming and fending off unwanted offers at Perlmutter's, and enjoying a delicious daily lunch at the drugstore down the street. The living-room set that my parents purchased on the installment plan is long gone, paid off, worn out, and eventually replaced, unlike Mom and Dad, who were only worn out. But I still have the hutch that opens up into a long dining-room table, an ingenious design that fascinated my father and impresses everyone that sees the innovative way it works. The finish marred and chipped from many decades of faithful service at extended family gatherings, I see now that it's not solid maple after all, only a thin veneer, an affordable piece better suited to Mom and Dad's modest income. It still lives a second life as a nice bookshelf and a handy writing desk, a quiet place to scribble in my journal and a tangible reminder of noisy family dinners, precious, hardworking parents, and my early life on the lowly bottom rung.

Carport

I've hit the jackpot. I'm not old enough for a learner's permit let alone a driver's license, but I own my own '64 Chevy Impala SS—silver blue with a white convertible top and whitewall tires mounted on Cragar super-sport steel wheels. I glance around the spacious, blue-vinyl interior and dream of driving. This wild ride boasts comfy front bucket seats, a faux-wood console, and a potent 327-cubic-inch V8 engine that's bored and stroked and crowned with a high-rise magnesium manifold and twin Holley four-barrel carburetors. I grasp the ivory-colored knob on the custom Hurst shifter, put the four-speed Muncie transmission into neutral, and then turn the key. The 365-plus horsepower engine roars like a snoring giant. I punch the gas pedal and awaken the angry titan, rocking the entire room; he's raring to get up and go, eager to release his energy out on the open road.

My friends claim that this magnificent machine once beat a Corvette Sting Ray off the line, and the story's likely true—even if they were under the influence of beer, bragging, and brainless enthusiasm at the time. After all, the infamous Norm Richter himself rebuilt the engine, and Richter knows auto mechanics. He also knows how to get his revenge: he empties his dirt-filled dump truck onto the hood of a parked state police car and drives off while the troopers are inside having a cup of coffee, nifty payback for a citation they gave him earlier for exceeding his load capacity.

Before becoming mine, this souped-up Impala belonged to Jimmy Zolini, a family friend and the former center on our undefeated football team. Jimmy graduates in '66, three years before I serve out my own sentence under the watchful eye of the New York State Board of Education. He then drops out of Duchess Community College and decides to join the Marines to avoid being drafted into the Army and sent to the front lines during the Vietnam War. I know that this doesn't make sense, but then neither does the Vietnam War. I'm sure this carefully calculated strategy for minimizing Jimmy's chances of suffering serious injury or death adds up when the recruiter persuades him to make the deal and sign his life on the dotted line. Oorah! Now he needs to persuade someone equally gullible that buying his hot car will decrease their chances of suffering serious injury or death. And I'm the man. I've already saved enough money to make a down payment, and I can pay off the balance in a year. We come to terms and his fantastic car is mine, all mine. Oorah!

I purchase the Impala with my own money, and I tell my parents I want the title in my own name—even though this means I'll pay much more for insurance. Dad tries to tell me it would make more sense to put the title in their name and insure it under their policy, but he respects my independent attitude, my need to be my own man and hold the title on my own vehicle. "If you're sure that's what you want to do," he says, granting consent while giving me a chance to change my mind. Fully insured but unlicensed and unprepared to go for a real ride, I pull the Impala in and out of the carport and jounce slowly down and back up our deeply rutted driveway. My skinny legs too weak to control the stiff clutch, I dog and stall the supercharged engine, which would rather howl down the open road. It's definitely way too much car for an absolute novice, and I quickly realize that I'm too anxious and too sensible to ever unleash its explosive power on a public roadway.

But it turns out that a parked Impala makes a good place to go parking. One evening my friend Tommy and his girlfriend Michelle fix me up with her cousin Carolyn, in town for a two-week visit. We just sit around the living room at first, doing next to nothing. Impatient with my shy inside manner and lack of moves, she suggests that I show her my cool car, but I'm just as cautious out in the dark carport. A complete neophyte, I figure we should get acquainted before we get physical; only I have no notion of what to say to this alien being beside me, the female form of the human species. I babble about the car, of course. I start the engine and turn it off again two or three times, stalling. I stare at my shoes for a few minutes and that leads to gibberish about how I match my socks with my shirt rather than with my pants, an awkward low point in a pitiful opening scene.

After a while, Tommy comes outside to see what's not going on, calls me from the car, and warns me that I had better cut all this slow-moving dialog and inject some real action into act two or else, and then he strides back to the house. I'm stunned and embarrassed beyond breathing. But I recompose what's left of my woeful self and finally overcome my stage fright. I lean across the console between the bucket seats and kiss a girl for the first time. Carolyn isn't shy at all since she's already fluent in the French tongue, physical touch being one of her three lust languages, along with receiving gifts, and acts of service, or so I gather from all the hot gossip I listen to later. Unlicensed and unprepared to go for a real ride, I confine our carport parking to a series of passionate kisses, even though I know she wants me to boldly go where other guys have gone before. But I'm just too concerned with consequences to put an ardent sex drive into high gear and push the limit on a four-lane freeway.

An arrogant high school linebacker and all-state wrestling champion, Tommy never pauses to ponder, to look before he leaps, having learned early in life that he who hesitates misses a tackle or a takedown or a conquest. Eat, drink, and be merry, for tomorrow we die. A few days later, I hear he takes Carolyn for a ride to her happy place, that they go all the way to never-never land, enjoying a close encounter of the third kind, the complete opposite of an out-of-body experience. I don't know how her life turns out—and she doesn't know that I eventually become a confident and loving marital lover—but Tommy dies of an overdose.

In the meantime, when Michelle becomes pregnant by her boyfriend Tommy, they drive down to Maryland to get married, only to find out she's old enough at eighteen but that he needs parental permission because he's just sweet sixteen. This story doesn't make any sense to me. Why wouldn't they know this beforehand? Naïve about late-night illegal abortions, I fail to figure out the real reason for their quick trip out of state. All I hear is Michelle lost the baby. And all I see is that my folks feel sorry for Michelle—who's afraid to turn to her own parents—and allow her and Tommy to stay in our downstairs rec room for a few days, screened off by drapes Dad rigs up to provide much-needed privacy during her recovery.

I consider the costs and my vague feelings and fears, and I realize that I'm not ready for all that goes with having a driver's license and owning a car, not the way things are, not from what I hear and already see for myself. I'm not ready to drive, let alone to drive this savage machine, this hot party-car with its monster engine and its big backseat. I'm not prepared to free myself from the restraints of responsibility, to leave home and let loose, to ride off into the dark, decadent night, drinking and driving, carousing and crashing. I soon decide to sell the once precious Impala. I park the car near the end of our driveway and place a for-sale sign in the windshield, facing Myers Corners Road. I paid only eight hundred dollars, well below book value, but I'm convinced it's worth at least fourteen hundred with its bored and stroked engine and its high-rise magnesium intake manifold and four-barrel Holley carburetors, and its Muncie transmission, Hurst shifter, and Cragar racing wheels.

Soon a guy stops and offers me twelve hundred dollars, the book value and close to what I want. I hold firm at fourteen hundred, pointing out all the custom features and expensive extras. When he sees I won't budge, Dad gently intervenes. He pulls me aside and urges me to take the twelve hundred, that it's a fair price. He explains that the extras may not make the car worth more and may even make it harder to sell. I'm confident the car is worth what I'm asking, so I tell Dad I'll bide my time until a buyer that recognizes its real value comes along and pays the full price. Dad shrugs and turns up his hands, raising his eyebrows and drawing his lips down in a faux frown. "All right, if that's what you want to do." I sense Dad's sorry that I'm going to live and learn the hard way. But he still refrains from infringing on my right to make my own decisions, hoping he's wrong, even if he knows that he's not. He turns toward the man with the money and makes his what're ya gonna do gesture, signaling the premature end of our encounter. The man walks away, disappointed that I won't listen to reason. Maintaining my take-it-or-leave-it attitude, I watch him drive off into the sunset, his twelve hundred dollars in tow.

I wait for weeks and no one else even stops to consider the car, let alone make an offer, and I soon lament the one that got away. Dad says nothing, just watches, standing on the sidelines, sympathetic. Another guy finally comes by and offers four hundred dollars, half what I paid and a third of the earlier offer I turned down. I conclude that half a bird in the hand is better than no birds in the bush and accept the measly four hundred bucks. I feel deflated. The car is gone, along with all the hard-earned money I spent to buy and insure it. We both know I made a big, expensive mistake, but Dad spares me the shame of pointing out the obvious. Perhaps he's remembering his own missed opportunities. I've heard his story about how he once refused a lucrative job offer to sell encyclopedias fulltime—the Harvard Classics, the Five-Foot Shelf of Books—a decision he regrets and a tale he tells all his life.

On the Road

As soon as I turn sixteen, Dad takes me to Poughkeepsie to get my driver's permit at the Department of Motor Vehicles, and I ace the written test with a perfect score. On our way back to the car, we witness a woman force her big sedan into a tight space by repeatedly pushing against two adjacent cars with her front and rear bumpers. Dad stands astounded, shakes his head, and mumbles "damn women drivers." I'm more worried about how hard she makes parallel parking look. Dad gives me a few basic lessons and then I sign up for the required driver's education course at the high school, an irksome experience for my poor instructor, Mr. Scary.

One morning I look down at the dashboard to check my speed. Eyes off the road for far too long, I drift out of my lane toward oncoming traffic. Another morning—not long after I fail the official road test for the first time—I take my turn behind the wheel, reset the seat and mirrors, look both ways, and begin to go. Mr. Scary hits his auxiliary brake before I pull out in front of a car I don't see coming. A little later, I stop at a stop sign, check carefully to make sure the coast is clear, and start to take off. Mr. Scary again hits his auxiliary brake before I pull out in front of another car that I don't see coming. "If you make one more mistake like that," he explodes, "you'll never drive a school vehicle again." "Failing that road test," he fumes, "was the best thing that ever happened to you"; and also, I suppose, to innocent drivers of invisible cars.

I fail the road test two more times before I eventually earn my driver's license. I don't remember what went wrong the time I took the test much too soon after smoking a joint at a friend's house. On my last disastrous effort at surviving the ordeal, I'm possessed by the spirit of that woman we saw push her sedan into a tight parking spot on the day I aced the written test. I awkwardly maneuver my car into position on a busy city street and make repeated misguided attempts to coax the vehicle into the space between two parked cars. Afraid that I'm going to hit the car behind me, the exasperated examiner grabs the steering wheel in a death grip and puts an end to my last misaligned assault. "That's okay, that's enough," he says, panting. I assume this means he sees no need for me to finish since I obviously know how to parallel park, so I'm confused at first when he then directs me to return to our point of departure rather than continue the road test. On the way back to his safe haven, the agitated examiner scribbles nervously on his clipboard. Now I begin to wonder. Is he adding my name to a blacklist of bad drivers? Recalling the surname of that bumper-wielding woman, the parallel parker par excellence? Making a personal note that it's high time to seek other employment, but not as a driver's education instructor?

I don't recall which family cars I drive on all these road tests, but I'm certain I take only vehicles I believe I can parallel park. The dark pink Plymouth would be too big and bulky for me to manage, with its fins that flare from the rear fenders, ready to fly into the future with just the push of a button—instead of a conventional shift lever attached to the steering column, it sports space-age, push-button automatic transmission controls on the dashboard. The deep purple '54 Plymouth convertible coupe lacks power steering, and it takes a muscular man or my determined mother to turn the wide steering wheel. It would be impossible for me to maneuver around a corner, let alone into a tight space between two parked cars. And I doubt the examiner would appreciate the musty passenger compartment or the leaky canvas top, a porous membrane during heavy rain showers— unless he wants to wash his hair while I'm driving, definitely a dangerous idea. The navy-blue Chevy Biscayne, a former police vehicle with white doors and trunk would also make an odd impression on an official state examiner—at least until after my parents save enough to have it painted all blue, a welcome relief for concerned neighbors wondering why the police make daily visits to our house, although I suppose they figure it's probably about my three younger brothers' bad behavior.

I finally manage to pass the road test and become a bona fide licensed driver. But by now I'm already eighteen, old enough to die in far-off Vietnam rather than on the roads of America. Or mature enough to go missing in action like my Uncle Mike, who wandered wounded for three weeks in the cold Korean winter, carrying a more seriously wounded buddy on his back, their hands and feet frostbitten. A lucky high draft number redeems me from a similar awful fate in the jungles of Southeast Asia. My future sister-in-law's then thirty-seven-year-old father isn't so fortunate. He's only two years away from retirement when his helicopter crashes during a 1970 rescue mission, missing in action until the federal government finally closes his case and a bodiless casket in 2002. His family finds the official account of what happened to him unconvincing, devoid of evidence—no remains and no identifying artifacts, nothing. In the meantime, he's awarded posthumous medals and his name is inscribed in the black granite of the Vietnam Veterans Memorial Wall.

A newly licensed driver, I'm safe at home minding my own business, free to roam the roads of my beloved Hudson Valley, to terrorize and be terrorized by my fellow independent citizens, adolescent adult Americans one and all. Later I ride down more distant roads and see open countryside and big cities all across these United States. Although I seldom parallel park, I maintain a truly excellent driving record for the next forty-five years—no accidents and only two tickets, one thirty-seven years ago, and another twenty-five years ago. But I never really learn to enjoy driving, especially at night. I don't see well at night and I find headlights blinding—so I usually just drive with my eyes closed. I do learn to enjoy and to appreciate the value of a closed garage over an open carport, the privacy and protection it provides, a safe enclosure for a wild Impala or for a more domesticated car. Only in a garage you can't just turn the key and start the engine and dream of driving—unless you want to end the adventure altogether, here and now.

Zettle's Little Garden

Zettle's Little Garden isn't the kind of place the police keep an eye on or that needs a bouncer to bounce out troublemakers. It's not a place where macho men arm-wrestle for pride or money; where you have a few too many drinks and get loud and obnoxious; where one mister tough guy throws another through a plate glass window; or where people fight out in the parking lot, the public meeting place for morons anonymous. A quiet restaurant and bar owned by a middle-aged couple from behind the Iron Curtain, Zettle's is a place where a man can sit and not think about a thing, like he doesn't have a care in the outside world; where two friends can share a beer and shoot pool for fun; where a couple can come and play songs on the jukebox at low volume; or couples on a double date, like when Tommy and his girlfriend Michelle set me up with her cousin Carolyn, and we go down to Zettle's for a few casual evenings out.

Zettle's is a place where they don't worry about getting you out because they need your table for their next customer. They want you to relax and stay awhile, have a nice time, and come again soon. It's a place where you can get a beer—and maybe a bite to eat—and enjoy quiet conversation. You talk and laugh in low voices so you don't disturb the other patrons, if there are any. You sip your beer, play an easygoing round of pool, and sit back down and nurse another beer, maybe play another round of pool. And it's an ordinary pool table like you have at home—there's no need to insert a fistful of quarters to get a rack of balls. There's also no need to show ID to prove you're eighteen and old enough to drink, mature enough to be drafted into the U.S. Army and die young in Vietnam. I guess Zettle's immigrant owners don't see any problem with young people having a few beers—just as long as you remember to exercise self-control and behave like a fully civilized adult, respectful of others and not too full of yourself.

Zosh serves as Zettle's host and bartender and waiter, chief cook and bottle washer, as my mother would say; although I suppose that's his wife in the kitchen making meals and doing the dishes since the restaurant occupies the back half of their house—a regular room furnished with four small tables and a home bar with two stools, bright and airy with big windows and white tile floors. Maybe it's his accent or limited English or bad experiences back in the old country, but Zosh wouldn't say shit if he had a mouthful, as my mother would say. He just stands behind the bar polishing glasses with his pristine dishcloth, a prickly day's growth on his gray face.

Zettle's remains my buddy Mike Pappocapella's secret place where he goes alone to have a home-cooked meal and his daily dose of beers, until he brings a few close friends along and introduces us to Zosh. I'm only fifteen and just beginning to drink beer, but I hate the horrible taste. I like sweet things and beer is big on bitter; and it leaves a vomity aftertaste in your mouth. They say beer is an acquired taste, but why would I want to acquire a taste for piss-colored, vomit-flavored carbonated water? I drink it anyway since I want to be one of the guys and to act grown up more than I don't really want to retch down this wretched fluid.

Mike also urges me to try some delicious goulash, but one whiff and a glance and I'm already nauseated. I like my foods separated and easy to identify. Maybe the green goulash reminds me of escarole, and my father once bounced my head in a bowl of boiled escarole when I wouldn't eat what was put in front of me, back when we still lived in New Jersey. He grew up during the depression when food was scarce, so he finds my refusals inconceivable, and we fall into an unpleasant pattern: Dad insists I clean my plate and I resist foods that turn my stomach. Dr. DeLucia, who delivered me—my mother was completely unconscious at the time—prescribes a tonic to stimulate my appetite, but I find the flat taste of the tonic unappealing. My appetite improves after we move to Wappingers, but I remain a picky eater into my mid-twenties, until my wife introduces me to a host of delicious but unfamiliar foods: homemade stew with fresh vegetables; corned beef and cabbage; cornbread, ham hocks, and beans; and stir-fried sweet and sour pork.

Early one evening, Mike and I head over to Zettle's for a couple of quiet drinks. We turn off Myers Corners Road and drive down the bumpy dirt lane that leads to our destination, our pickup truck twisting and turning and rocking and rolling as we wind our way through a dense grove of tall trees with thick trunks, bare of lower branches and underbrush. We park at the edge of the grove and walk from the woods into a sunny, grass-covered clearing, our pupils dilating in the sunlight as we stroll toward the back entrance of a small white house—Zettle's Little Garden. Later that night, Mike and I are sipping our beers and chewing the fat together, and this middle-aged, scruffy-looking man who's had a few too many keeps sticking his nose in and making rude remarks, trying to stir up trouble. We ignore his insults until he becomes so obnoxious and annoying and in our faces that Mike puts him firmly in his place; that's the end of that—he shuts up and keeps to himself, although I soon realize that he's sitting there fuming and imagining his revenge.

Later I'm outside in the dark woods standing near the truck, waiting for Mike to complete his pit stop in the restroom before we head home, and loudmouth man appears out of nowhere and warns me that he's going to get Mike. He marches off and returns waving a large hammer over his head. When he takes an awkward swing in my direction, I grab the hammer by the long handle, yank it from his weak grip, and toss it into the dense forest. He scampers after it as though we're playing fetch and I'm the master and he's my mangy dog. Then it sinks into my head that this guy means business—so I catch up before he can retrieve his hammer and return for round two. I'm not sure what I should do, but I've heard Mike's stories about his big fights and about brawls that he's seen, so I imagine this is my moment, time to make my own story, time to put up or shut up, time to be the kind of guy my friends admire. Hammer man's in no shape to hit me, but I rain blows down upon his frail body, a hailstorm beating against the umbrella of his older arms, raised to shelter his head and protect his torso, and he crumples to the ground, crushed like a cardboard box.

I reach down and pick up the hammer and throw it through the air, hurtling past tree trunks like it's Thor's divine thunder weapon flying through a Norse forest. Only I'm not a good god, defending the right, protecting the people, healing their hurts. I'm a brute, panting and fully of fury, too agitated to see that it's time to stop, too full of mythic stories bloated with boasting, too naïve to know that they're a bunch of baloney, exaggerated representations of reality. And I do a dastardly deed—I kick a man when he's down. I kick him hard in the side and back with the toe of my leather shoe, without a care for the damage I might inflict on his bruised body. I kick him again. I start toward the truck but turn back and kick him one more time for good measure. I leave him lying on the forest floor and return to the truck.

Mike finally finishes his business and comes out into the darkness. When I tell him about what happened, he just says we should get going. I guess we figure the guy will get up and go home once we're gone. As I describe the details and also later when Mike relates his big-fish version of the story, trumpeting my supposed prowess in battle, he whacks me hard on the shoulder, saying way to go, and all that triumphant American jazz. No need to blow my own horn, which would sound a sour note now anyway, totally out of tune with what's happening in my heart. A few days later, Mike says he's been to Zettle's and Zosh told him that I shouldn't come back, that I'm no longer welcome, that the injured man was taken to the hospital with several cracked ribs. I feel like a lowlife, guilty and embarrassed that I hurt the poor guy when it wasn't necessary, when he was too drunk to defend himself. And I'm sad to be cast out of Zettle's Little Garden for my bad behavior. I wonder how Zosh even knows about the ugly incident. Did the man come inside, seeking assistance? Did he find him lying on the ground? Did the police come by, asking questions?

Mike continues to enjoy Zettle's hospitality and their hot Hungarian goulash, dropping by alone to imbibe his daily dose of beers. I ride past the little unpaved private road that leads to the sunny, grass-covered clearing in the dense woods, but I never return to the little restaurant and bar with its bright and airy room. I never again play a peaceful game of pool or watch Zosh polish glasses at the bar. And soon enough I quit drinking piss-colored, vomit-flavored carbonated water that leaves a nasty aftertaste in my mouth. I don't know what happens to hammer man, but Mike dies young decades later—after losing a lifelong battle with one too many beers.

Trade Winds

I'm underage and I need a willing stranger's ID to sail into the Trade Winds, a large bar and restaurant between Newburgh and Stewart Air Force Base, on the far side of the expansive Hudson River. Tommy borrowed a friend's ID, and Mark and Jimmy are over eighteen, old enough to drink and eligible for the draft, mature enough to disturb the peace at home and to make war in faraway lands. I hand my supposed driver's license to the big guy guarding the door. He looks from the photo to my face. There's a definite resemblance: we both have brown hair, two eyes, two ears, one nose, and one empty head, and we're both about the same height and weight, give or take four inches and forty pounds. I barely look old enough to ride a bicycle let alone drive a car after dark, but the bouncer isn't authorized to require a road test; I just need to know my own birthdate. I'm turned away on the first few tries—until I get all my ducklings and my fictitious birthday in a row—and also the right bouncer. I don't recall numbers very well, and I'm a terrible liar. And I guess you need to know how to lie through your teeth with a straight face before you can finally be considered a full-fledged adult, ready to contribute to a sick society, to conspire and conquer in the corporate world, to scheme and prevail in the political arena, and to deceive and vanquish the enemy in Vietnam.

You also need to know how to hold your liquor, as the old saying goes, yet another of my many adolescent inadequacies. Jimmy, Mark, and Tommy drink beer, a more down-to-earth but less intoxicating beverage, but I go for sweeter, more potent concoctions, and after a couple of Screwdrivers, I veer into other tables on the long voyage to the toilet, and I have a hard time tacking my way back to the dock. I'm lost in Phog, our favorite local band, listening to loud rock music and watching Sal D'Addario play his bass guitar, his Italian-American Afro amplifying his head as he bobs and weaves, boxing out the beat. But I still notice a mild commotion at the next table. Mark has moved over to arm-wrestle this Russian guy, and a group of onlookers has gathered to urge them on. Mark wins without burning more than a couple of calories, amused by the effort of his pushover adversary, his teeth clenched, his face red, his neck taut, trying to defeat a former enemy.

We smile and shake our heads, knowing what the poor guy is up against. An award-winning, all-state offensive tackle, catcher, and point guard, widely recognized around the region for his prowess on the football field, baseball diamond, and basketball court, Mark has big biceps, powerful forearms, beefy shoulders, a deep chest, true grit, and a pleasant, easygoing personality; plus he's a popular lover of young ladies, so I'm surprised when he tells me that the ultimate experience would be inexperience, to not have sex until after marriage and then to marry a girl who has also never been to the promised land. The Russian makes a few more fruitless attempts at arm-wrestling, pushing with all his strength, struggling hard against an immovable object, but Mark triumphs again and again, a twinkle in his eye and a playful smile on his winsome face. He refrains from laughing out loud.

Rather than just admit defeat, the loser decides to change the challenge to a weightlifting contest, so we pile into cars, drive into town, and sneak into his brother's basement. The whole family's sound asleep upstairs, so no loud cheering for the champions during their struggle. Downstairs in a large exercise room, Mark and the Russian do a series of deadlifts, adding weights until the load reaches several hundred pounds, raising and then dropping a massive barbell with a big boom. All of a sudden the door flies open and this huge muscular man ducks through the open doorway and interrupts the contest. We've awakened the Angry Red Giant, and he's as outraged as Nikita Khrushchev banging his shoe on a table at the UN and vowing we will bury you. Fortunately, he's a Russian defector working for the U.S. Air Force now, shoeless and in pajama bottoms; unfortunately, he's on the side of peace and quiet for his family.

The Angry Red Giant wants to know what the hell we think we're doing, yelling at his younger brother to get us out of there, but younger brother wants a few more minutes to win the weightlifting competition. The Angry Red Giant quickly ends the argument with immediate action. He snatches the heavy barbell with one hand and tosses it aside like it's a prop for a play, demanding we quit playing with these toys and get out of his house. He raises his arm to wave us away, but we're already retreating toward the door, kowtowing and apologizing, hoping to leave with our lives and no broken bones. We hustle into the car, slam the doors, and hurtle down the driveway, our souped-up '64 Impala eager to escape the roaring beast in the basement. As the car peels out onto the road, tires shrieking, we shout out our shock and awe. "Holy shit, did you see that guy?" "Did you see him toss that barbell with only one hand?" "Unbelievable."

We leave the town that housed the headquarters of General Washington's ragtag Continental Army and retreat across the Newburgh–Beacon Bridge, recently erected to replace the ferry, the fouled Hudson River far below, clogged central artery of a heavenly valley, poisoned by oil pollution, toxic chemicals, and raw sewage. We head toward Beacon, longtime home of Pete Seeger, world-famous folksinger and protester par excellence, and advocate for liberty and life, for freedom of speech and assembly, for social and economic justice, worldwide peace, and clean water. The bright lights of Beacon signal that we're not far from home now, safe and sound on our own side, back where the future awaits: the eventual end of the Vietnam War, the fall of the Berlin Wall, the opening up of the Iron Curtain, the dissolution of the old Soviet Union; the rebirth of the historic Hudson River, Pete Seeger's sloop Clearwater sailing from port to port, promoting the health and renewal of the waterway; widespread approval after decades of condemnation for his courageous refusal to respond to un-American questions from the House Committee on Un-American Activities, questions about singing popular folksongs for audiences denounced by the federal government, revolutionary anthems like "This Land Is Your Land" and "If I Had a Hammer."

I can't say I returned from our trip across the river wiser than I was before. But I now see I shouldn't disturb a person's peace, I shouldn't wake a family man in the middle of the night, I shouldn't give him cause to act like an Angry Red Giant. I see that I should show proper respect and allow him his freedom, the freedom to enjoy his life, his liberty, and his land, to pursue his happiness. And I see that if I have the hammer of justice and the bell of freedom and know the song about love between my brothers and my sisters, that I should hammer out danger, ring out a warning, and sing out love, all over this land—this land that was made for you and me, for the grandson of Italian immigrants and for a Russian defector from the Soviet Union, fleeing from poverty and oppression and hoping for freedom and opportunity.

Points of Order

We're quietly working on our geometry problems one ordinary boring day in the twelfth grade, when Harry Schultz decides he should put a sharper point on his pencil. After all, it never hurts to have a sharp point on your pencil when you're trying hard to apply a dull mind to a perplexing problem. Even Harry knows that, and he's not the sharpest tack in the box, so he does what any ordinary human being would ordinarily do under ordinary circumstances. He gets up from his desk, walks to the front of the room, puts his pencil in the pencil sharper, and cranks the handle. Harry doesn't realize or has apparently forgotten that these aren't ordinary circumstances and you therefore don't do what ordinary people would ordinarily do when they want to sharpen an ordinary pencil. This is Mrs. Patutti's classroom and she has her reasonable rules against people sharpening pencils without permission.

Carefree and oblivious, Harry removes his razor-sharp pencil from the pencil sharpener, blows the sawdust off, and turns halfway around, ready to return to his seat. At precisely this point, an indignant Mrs. Patutti rises to make her own point, pushing her old wooden chair back with her big bottom, the screech along the floor a warning that Harry doesn't heed. Her short, blonde curls jumping, the hefty battleax bowls toward Harry's frail body and initiates her Italian American version of the Spanish Inquisition. "What do you think you're doing?" she demands in a vexed voice, her angry glare magnified by her scuba-mask eyeglasses.

"Sharpening my pencil," Harry offers, contrite but woefully ignorant of the gravity of his sin and the inadequacy of his answer, unaware that his transgression calls for a complete public confession and that this is therefore the wrong response. Judgment is swift and the punishment immediate. The Grand Inquisitor takes an ample backswing and lets loose and whacks Harry sharply upside his empty head. The blow sends his thick eyeglasses flying across the room, hurtling toward his seat, an odd way to tell him where to go. But this is geometry, and in this orderly place the shortest distance between two points is a straight line. And a student at rest should remain at his desk until granted permission to rise and sharpen his pencil, the laws of motion also an integral part of the rule-governed realm of Mrs. Patutti's classroom.

I wouldn't want to give mean Mrs. Patutti an excuse for her high-and-mighty manner, but I must admit that maybe there's something about Harry Schultz that makes some people want to unload on him. I mean I beat him up myself on the school bus one day, and I'm not one to beat people up. Well, not counting the time I beat up Willie Schneider at his bus stop or the time I beat up my best friend Richie Weston in the school hallway at Wappingers Junior High, years before being ushered into the elegant, well-ordered world of plane geometry.

~*~

Mrs. Patutti may feel free to put her hands on Harry Schultz, but I doubt that she would try to pull a stunt like that on a less

109

fainthearted fellow, someone ready, willing, and able to defend his rights, somebody bold enough to take a stand and make his own point of order—my brother Robert, for instance. But Robert would certainly never strike a woman, an attitude he likely acquired from our mother, who gives this warning to anyone who even thinks about raising a hand to her: "Don't you dare, I'll break it off and hit you with the bloody end." And yet he wouldn't let mean Mrs. Make a Point slap him upside the head either. Robert's faster than a greased lightning bolt, and her dodged blow would miss him and hit her infamous pencil sharpener, leaving her point of order unmade, nullified by his nifty maneuver.

On the other hand, Robert doesn't grant full immunity to any male teachers that might go too far to press a point of order—unfortunately for Mr. Rotten Egg Breath. One fateful afternoon, he sees Robert wandering unfettered in the hallway and he tries his puny hand at that advanced teacher-intimidation technique where they get in your face and launch into a stern lecture a few inches from your nose. No timid Harry Schultz, Robert isn't easily intimidated, not even by hellacious halitosis. Inspired by the indomitable spirit and the audacious actions of the American colonists, he declares his independence and fights for his unalienable, God-given rights to life, liberty, the pursuit of happiness, and access to the school corridors. He seizes this tyrannical agent of foreign power by the front of his shirt, slams him into a locker, and walks off. We're no longer subject to the Spanish Inquisition or the British Crown; we're in post-sixties America, land of the free and home of the rebellious, where respect for abuse of authority isn't what it used to be.

Fortunately for both these bad-boy authority figures, Robert had stopped biting people long before he entered high school, but he retains a lifelong oral fixation. Born with three teeth, by the time he's three-years-old, he possesses a mouthful of razor-sharp weapons, a stealthy attack style, and an excruciating bite. His victims never know he's near until they hear their own voice emit a bloodcurdling scream as his teeth pinch the top layers of skin on the back of an upper thigh. If they do hear him coming, kids as old as twelve flee, frantically warning everyone within earshot: "It's Robert, it's Robert, run, run." I doubt, however, that Robert intends to make a point of order at this early age. I suppose that he's simply exercising his unalienable right to life, liberty, and the sweet pleasures of vampirism. Born to bite and ready to remind the bigger kids on the block not to ignore their inferiors, I imagine he's just fulfilling his divine purpose—make the high-and-mighty painfully aware that you can't keep the little people down forever, for they will eventually rebel and find an effective way to make their presence felt.

Auto Motive

My first day in the auto shop at Barker's, a big department store down in Fishkill, I lock a customer's keys in the trunk of his car. My good friend Mike Pappocapella tries and tries to jimmy the latch, but without any luck. He decides that we should detach the backseat to gain access from inside the vehicle, and as we wrestle the bulky seat away from the back wall of the passenger compartment, we accidentally tear the interior roof above the rear window. It's just a tiny rip in an out-of-the-way spot, so we don't say anything to anyone, hoping the customer won't notice. I guess Mike wants to keep his reputation intact—although he leaves a few weeks later for a better position and a chance to escape before it's too late and I ruin his good name, before the manager remembers that Mike is the one that got me this job at the shop where he works fulltime as an auto mechanic.

Another day I drain the oil from a customer's car and change the filter but forget to refill the engine with fresh oil. Luckily, the driver discovers my blunder before his engine seizes up and requires a complete overhaul; and Dave, the assistant manager, doesn't fire me or even report the incident to the manager. But everyone whispers and wonders, and I can almost hear their heads shaking. I don't see whether they're also laughing up their sleeves since my eyes are fixed on the floor. During a different evening shift, I remove the oil filter and unscrew the plug from the oil pan, let the old oil drain out, and install a new filter. But when I attempt to replace the plug—before refilling the engine with fresh oil—I'm unable to turn the plug with my fingers before tightening with an adjustable wrench. I don't see that the plug's going in on an angle, I just assume my fingers are too weak for the task, so I grab a wrench and crank and crank and crank and crank until I cross-thread the plug and ruin the oil pan. Fortunately, one of the mechanics is able to rethread the pan and repair the damage, at a cost of considerable time but no cash money.

Dave still doesn't fire me or bother to report the incident to the manager, but he does decide it would be wise to limit me to changing tires and repairing flats, although this also involves a calculated risk. I must remember to replace and tighten the lug nuts so I don't send a car out the door with its wheels ready to fly off and roll down the road on their own. And I must also avoid cross-threading a lug nut and ruining an axle. Besides, now I'm also grappling with power tools, a raucous ratchet gun driven by a noisy air compressor that disrupts my concentration and my daydreams, imaginative flights of fancy about girls I fancy. No wheels fall off and I don't cross-thread any lug nuts, but I'm not strong enough or mechanically-inclined enough to repair flats and to change tires without constant bailouts from more capable coworkers. My father might win cash awards at IBM for his many suggestions on how to improve their business machines and production practices, but I sure didn't inherit his mechanical mind. And I might like reading hot rod magazines and building custom model cars; I might have a new engine block in my bedroom and a souped-up Chevy Impala out in our carport, but I'm a fish out of water in an auto shop, drowning in an alien atmosphere.

Dave still doesn't dismiss me or suggest a different line of work; he simply arranges for me to switch places with the stock boy. I suppose he thinks that I'll be significantly safer inside the department store and much less likely to cost the company a fortune for a bodily injury lawsuit or for repairs to damaged vehicles. And perhaps he also hopes that I'll be a lot less likely to witness the boatloads of automotive products going out the garage bay doors and into his trunk and into the trunks of all our coworkers, a misguided attempt to supplement their meager salaries with an unauthorized fringe benefit. I soon see what's happening and laugh along when I hear hushed stories that boast about how one guy ripped off entire cases of everything from soup to nuts. I agree to go along when Dave asks me to keep quiet, but I feel bad knowing that they're robbing the place blind, and lonely in my silent, lily-livered honesty. Ironically, I'm the one accused of stealing from the department store.

It's my break and Dave asks me to pick up some coffee for the crew while I'm at the diner next door for a big cup of hot chocolate. As I weave through Barker's, I stop to look at record albums for a few minutes on my way out, and when I reach the front door a plainclothes security guard takes me upstairs to the office and accuses me of having an album hidden underneath my zipped-up army jacket. I tell them I work in the automotive department and that I'm on my break. They demand that I open my jacket, and I comply. Dumbfounded I don't have a stolen record in my possession, they say I must have hidden it in the store before they could catch up with me. I insist that I haven't taken anything, but they don't believe me. They warn that they'll be watching and then they turn me loose. I guess I'm presumed guilty until proven innocent, a major hallmark of the American criminal injustice system.

My break's long over when I finally return to the automotive department, shamefaced and empty-handed. When Dave wants to know where I've been all this time and why I don't have the coffee, I relate what happened with our overzealous defenders of imaginary record albums. He's pissed off and protective, indignant that they would stop and search one of his guys like that. He'll get the coffee, but first he's going to the office to straighten them out. Dave hesitates a moment to ask if I stole the record album, drawing collusively close and lowering his voice and eyes like it's okay, he won't tell anyone. I say no and he asks if I'm sure. Convinced by my sincere denials, he's ready to read them the riot act, as my mother would say, confident that he's not talking through his hat. Relieved I have nothing to confess, I still feel nervous about getting into trouble, what with security watching and ready to render another false accusation.

I like stocking shelves better than working in the shop. It's clean and quiet, and I'm able to do a decent job with less stress. It's like working at the Wagon Wheel Deli, except I don't deal with customers; Debra, the nice girl who runs the register does that. When I'm back in the stockroom, Dave often makes snide remarks about her lack of good looks and about her being a good girl. But I like her, and I like having a female friend to talk to when we're not busy, especially since she's a few years wiser and makes me feel better about myself.

But I absolutely detest talking and working with Jeff, the auto department manager, whenever he decides to stay for my five-to-ten nightshift. He's odd and disorganized, unreliable, and a weak leader. His clothes are all rumpled, he doesn't bathe often enough, and his hair and teeth look like he lost his comb and his toothbrush ages ago. I now recognize maybe these were signs of depression or a drinking problem or personal turmoil, maybe a troubled marriage or recent divorce, grounds for concern not contempt. Jeff doesn't want me to stand around talking to the cashier even when we have nothing to do, no customers to take care of or shelves to stock. He assigns me boring busy work, mindless tasks that make my five-hour shift flow like molasses in winter, transforming my eighteen thousand seconds into an eternity. I'm frustrated, but I understand why he would want me to keep busy while I'm on the clock.

What I definitely don't understand but deeply resent is that Mr. Magnificent Manager hardly ever pays us on time, another reason no one likes him. We're all sick and tired of this bullshit, and I'm about to blow my top. We still haven't received our checks again this pay period and Jeff keeps saying they should be here soon. Then on Friday night we hear that the daytime crew and members of the evening crew that started before five were paid in cash, that Jeff borrowed the money from the main store. The rest of us don't receive a dime. The office is closed now and we'll just have to wait until our checks finally arrive in the mail, but not until after the weekend is over.

I stew for the remainder of my shift, a fiery tirade for my incompetent manager simmering in my mind, bubbling beneath the surface at a low, slow boil. When my long shift comes to a close, I quickly remove the lid, ready to release the peppery rant I've rehearsed all evening. I insist on my money and Jeff says there's nothing he can do. We go back and forth and he won't budge or show any sympathy. I launch a cruel personal attack, yelling and swearing a blue streak, firing verbal bullets like I've already been drafted into the army, issued an M-16 rifle, and shipped to Vietnam to fight for truth, justice, and the American way. I look up to see a crowd of customers gawking, my fiery mouth-grenades exploding in their ears, and I see Dad coming across the store, here to pick me up from work.

Dad's too late to settle me down and his initial attempts to talk sense remain unheard, but he appears to appreciate that I'm only insisting on my right to be paid. I'm already fully enflamed, so incensed I grab an empty gas can and threaten to smash Jeff in the head if he doesn't pay me now. Dad intervenes, standing between me and my manager, who looks like an enemy soldier with his hands on his head and a gun thrust into his face. Dad's calming voice finally defuses my f-bombs and verbal bullets and my attempted assault fizzles. I'm out of emotional ammunition, exhausted. The incident ends in a Vietnam-style standoff. Jeff fires me and I quit. He gives me fifteen dollars and I pick up the balance of my outstanding wages a few days later, another fat fifty dollars for a two-week pay period.

Now out of work, I miss having money to go to concerts and to listen to live bands at the Trade Winds and the Coral Reef; money for mixed drinks and Mexican marijuana; money for record albums—since I definitely don't steal them, imaginary evidence to the contrary. But I don't miss the boring work or Jeff's body odor and bad breath. I don't miss working until ten every weekday night with school starting the next morning and me trying to hang on for a few more months until graduation. And it's really nice to have time for more important matters— like listening to rock music, smoking marijuana in a water pipe, and pondering my uncertain future. Will I graduate from high school? Will I get to go to California, where what's happening is happening? Will I flee to Canada if I'm cursed with a low draft number in the lottery that determines the destiny of eligible eighteen-year-olds, or will I end up in Vietnam? Will I survive the rumble in the jungle, or will I return in a pine box draped in the good old red, white, and blue—the colors of the ripe blood I bled, of the pale-faced fear I felt, and of the melancholy mood of those left to mourn my loss.

I Almost Went to Woodstock

I'm dazed and confused, adrift in a purple haze, trying to find myself and my place in a weird adult world that disturbs my uneasy mind—a world where atomic bombs threaten our very existence; where war rages on in Southeast Asia; where tanks and armored vehicles violate our urban streets; where race riots disrupt our cities; where armed police officers attack peaceful protesters; where industrialism destroys our land, water, and air; where materialism consumes our communities; where greedy corporations grab for economic advantage; where the lust for a life of ease overwhelms our inner desires for life, liberty, and the pursuit of real happiness; where corrupt and ignorant politicians seek their own twisted aims and fail to form a more perfect union, establish justice, insure domestic tranquility, promote the general welfare, and secure the blessings of liberty for every inhabitant of this lovely land.

My increasing alienation from society—my turn-on, tune-in, and drop-out attitude—has been building for months, escalating during my senior year and reaching its climax in the summer of

'69; my first summer free from a mind-numbing industrialized school system modeled after the modern prison; the summer of the miracle Mets and the lunar landing; the summer I almost went to Woodstock, looking for love, enlightenment, and peace, for longed-for association and acceptance, for communion and community.* I feel myself a child of God, walking along the road, going on down to Yasgur's farm; going to join in a rock and roll band, going to camp out on the land, going to try to get my soul free. I feel myself a cog in something turning. Maybe it's the time of year or maybe it's just the time of man. I don't know who I am, but I know life is for learning. I know we are stardust, we are golden, we are billion-year-old carbon, caught in the devil's bargain; and we've got to get ourselves back to the garden. I dream of bombers, riding shotgun in the sky, turning into butterflies above our nation, and everywhere there is song and celebration.

While I wait and yearn for a better day, I drag myself to classes and struggle to adjust to the hippie counterculture both in and out of school. I skip classes and stay home or come to my morning history class high on hashish. I do enough work to keep from failing, but I'm at odds with the fetching twenty-two-plus Miss Prissy, who isn't pleased that I'm drowsy from my morning toke and bored by her dry lectures. But I often revive and achieve a more alert condition, roused by her stirring visual aids. I pay rapt attention when she turns toward the blackboard, her ample ass to the class, and I awaken when her round breasts quiver as she pounds her historical pulpit at climactic moments in her presentation.

I'm far too uncomfortable and embarrassed by my awkward attempts to adopt the groovy new look to fall asleep anyway. I keep my chin on my chest and my eyes down the day I wear a bright blue shirt with a huge collar and big red polka dots, gray flannel pants with enormous bellbottoms flared from the knee, an extra-wide cranberry-colored paisley belt, and a pair of black Beatle-boots. Thank God there aren't any photographs, but I

119

haven't checked every odd curiosity collection or offbeat wax museum in America. I only wear that garish clown shirt a few times—all I need is a bulbous red nose and I'm ready to run away and join the Ringling Bros. and Barnum & Bailey Circus. But I quickly learn to love flowing down the hall in those flared bellbottoms, the opposite of what I wore last year—skin-tight, peg-leg pants, real crotch-grabbers, an unintended form of male birth control you pry over your heels with a shoehorn. I also learn to sport a pair of trip glasses when occasion calls; with prism lenses, they're a real trip—except when you look out the window and envision a dozen cop cars and there's actually only one—that's a real bummer.

I lost my job months ago and I only bother with homework when it's unavoidable, so I have lots of time to appreciate the mind-expanding rhythms and melodies of rock music and to puff on my water pipe, ensconced in my dark, windowless basement bedroom. Navy blue drapes decorated with screen-printed white flowers cover one entire wall of my psychedelic den, cloaking the clothes closet, the flowers all aglow under an intense blacklight. When smoking marijuana makes me crave cake and cookies, I steal upstairs to our well-stocked kitchen and swallow platefuls of sweet treats; when it makes me sleepy, I take prolonged afternoon naps, drifting far away from our adulterated adult society, gone to Neverland. But I never escape karma and achieve nirvana. I always return to face my fate in this fallen old world—figure out how to grow up without losing what's left of my childhood soul; how to keep my spirit alive and my mind and heart open; how to actually achieve a higher consciousness without losing my mind and abusing my body; how to be a head and still keep my head.

On weekends, we go to shows and check out the chicks and the best rock bands, looking for foxy ladies and listening to live music at a host of local venues—city parks and school gyms, the Belly of the Whale below the Catholic Church, a forgotten place in Poughkeepsie close to Vassar College, and the Trade

Winds and the Coral Reef, restaurant clubs across the Hudson River. I'm entranced when Electric Bike's lead guitarist sings and plays the same notes simultaneously, like Jimi Hendrix on Voodoo Chile. Storm's blues-style bass player blows my mind: his fingers move like lightning and a flashflood of pulsating sound inundates the outdoor arena, punctuated with syncopated thunder; a shower of sixteenth notes pelts the ground, and it's as if it's raining buckets full of sunshine. And I'm amazed when Spider swings up from New York City for a truly professional-level performance, the band totally tight and on the beat, lead guitar screaming, crying, weeping, drum kit rocking and rolling through multiple harmonious rhythms.

But what turns me off is the way so many event organizers instruct all their employees to hassle anyone hanging around outside without buying a ticket or paying the advance cover charge, afraid they might sneak in and see the show for free. One night, I'm at a local high school and I've been inside and paid for a ticket, and now I'm out on the lawn for a break, for fresh air and quiet conversation with friends. And this bozo bouncer's checking to see if everyone has a stamp on their hand to prove they've paid, and he's telling them to leave if they don't have a damn stamp. Anyway, we're sitting on the ground, and when Mr. Bozo asks to see the back of my hand, I ignore him but mumble, "I've paid." He insists that I show him the stamp that authorizes my profane presence, and I insist that my word is good, that I'm telling you that I paid. He's getting all uptight, but I keep a cool head as we repeat our refrains, his demand for visual evidence versus my verbal testimony.

When I've had a bellyful of all this nonsense and sense a dramatic moment, I finally relent and reveal my hand. Everyone imagines I'm lying since I'm so insistent, that perhaps I doth protest too much. And everybody knows that I'm in trouble when my bare hand becomes visible, the bouncer ready to read me the riot act and expel me from the premises. But when he sees the infamous stamp plain as day, his face falls blank and his whole body loses life, like someone suddenly let the air out of a Joe Palooka punching bag. I didn't mean to humiliate the man, just make an important point; after all, the guy's just doing his job and doesn't deserve to be deflated. I only want my word to be accepted, to be taken at face value, to be believed by adults. I only want to be presumed honest until proven untrustworthy. And I want to be free peaceably to assemble and secure in my person against unreasonable searches. I mean why can't they just check people at the door, for crying out loud; why don't they read the Constitution of the United States and respect our individual civil rights. (I guess Miss Prissy's visual aids also help make her American history lectures more memorable.)

The bouncer goes back to his business of bothering other innocent people, and we all sit absolutely quiet, stunned by how well I handled what happened, by the extraordinary way I was in that amazing moment. And all of a sudden I get this huge rush—but I'm not high, haven't had anything at all, and it's not like any rush I've ever had when I'm high. I perceive an odd swirling inside my soul and all around, the air supercharged with an invigorating current, my mind and my body bursting with enlightening energy. I feel myself floating and sense the earth suspended in eternity. I divine myself here on this earth, in this body, aware that I'm an integral part of the peaceful presence of an all-encompassing everything. It's a genuine mystical moment, completely unexpected, an actual otherworldly experience.

When we aren't at public happenings, we go to house parties and get high while the host's parents are away, music blasting in the background. Married with a baby boy, Mark's friend Buddy Miller works for a mortician and rents a house with his wife. He's apparently brain-damaged from smoking grass soaked in formaldehyde. I guess that's why he thinks that it's cool to blow mouthfuls of marijuana smoke into his baby's face, oblivious when we all grimace and turn away. But Buddy just laughs and flashes what my mother would call a shit-eatin' grin, showing off his horrible teeth, the enamel eroded by amphetamines and cocaine. Almost always in a good mood, our happy host serves his homemade brownies mixed with marijuana. I politely wave away the treats and feel sad about the baby. This isn't my kind of party. And Buddy's not my kind of guy—even though he really is a nice guy, just messed up, his mind way out of whack.

Another night I'm tripping out on Blue Cheer, the best LSD around—much more pleasant than Witches Brew, a concoction more likely to lead to a bad trip or to being chased by trees—and we decide I should stay overnight at a friend's house so that I won't I be left alone while I'm still high on acid. My friend falls asleep, of course, and I'm left alone after all. Only instead of resting in my familiar, comfortable room at home, I'm stuck without a bed in an unfinished basement, amid a scattering of odds and ends—including a toy log cabin made of sheet metal that keeps calling me. I'm intrigued by the enigma of the cabin and its closed front door, by the mystery of the world evoked by its existence, by the compelling question of what might be going on inside. I stare for a long time, my mind fixed on this odd artifact, drawn to a dark brown mark on the beige front door that I can't quite distinguish from far across the room, by the light of one small bulb fixed in the unfinished ceiling. I gaze until I finally find my focus, my vision traveling to the cabin and back, and at last I see the mark become a Christian cross, a sure sign of God's presence.

I hear this nonverbal signal in my newly opened heart, and it makes me marvel. I wonder why in the world would a toy log cabin have a cross on its closed front door, a redeeming riddle that occupies my mind until the early morning light replaces the sacred relic with the image of an article more congruent with the little log cabin—it's only a horseshoe hanging there, a rustic decoration nailed to the enigmatic entrance. Of course the cross no longer appears, a ghost gone away with the night, returned to its own endless lifeworld, to a place beyond this mundane, dingy basement. I see this sign as evidence presented and taken away, case closed, leaving me as the only eyewitness of a momentary manifestation; the grateful recipient of a private gift granted to bring back my once more believing mind, freeing me from the doubts I developed over the last few years after I failed to find adequate answers to my questions about the mysteries of life.

~*~

In the meantime, we drive down to New Jersey one weekend for a visit. I don't want to go because it's boring and because my crude maternal grandfather has an intolerant attitude and a loud mouth. He's the very hard-working head custodian for the Paterson school district, and a caring, good guy in his own old-fashioned way—he once gave me a beautiful bicycle left too long in the lost and found. But I suppose all he learned from his own unpleasant experience with prejudice was to change his surname so people couldn't tell that he was Italian; after all, he was born in America, albeit nearly two decades before women's suffrage and several years before the constitutional amendment authorizing income taxes. I come anyway to placate my parents, especially my mother, but I bring along a chunk of bad attitude, a chip on my shoulder big enough for Paul Bunyan.

We arrive at my grandparents' house in Hawthorne, and my grandfather feels compelled to question my long hair and my masculinity. "What d'ya squat to pee?" he asks, insinuating an insult, but I bite my tongue and tell him no, turning my head and averting my eyes to avoid any overt sign of disrespect or defiance. "I suppose you smoke marijuana too," he continues, pushing his agenda and my buttons. I don't know whether he actually wants a response, if this is a question or his conclusion, but I'm unashamed of my answer, plus I see a good chance for payback. I say yes, confirming his worst fears. He's dumbstruck and deflated, the starch gone out of his shorts, as both he and my mother would say. I don't dare watch, but I hear him walk away, muttering to himself like an alienated madman.

I feel bad but it's too late to take back. I've gone too far—I should have left his rhetorical question alone; I should have left the poor man in peace. He suffers his first heart attack a few days later. I know it's not my fault that he's so damn uptight, that I'm not personally responsible for his reaction, that he just doesn't understand, that he has antiquated ideas about rebelling against the status quo, even if his own life isn't exactly a picnic under the current system. But I clearly contributed to his heart attack. I gave him real cause for his concern. Mom asks if I said anything to Grandpa, that Grandma says he was so upset after we left, that he kept saying to himself, "No, no, not Richard, no, not Richard," that he just couldn't believe it. I lie and deny and practice pleading the fifth, feigning ignorance like some pitiful politician that refuses to confirm or deny reports about irregular government activities.

Later this same summer, I'm expected around midnight one weekend but stroll in about ten the next morning without a word, looking for a little breakfast. Dad calmly tries to make me aware of their worry, holding his tongue and temper for Mom's sake and mine. I shrug him off, signifying that I'm my own man and I'll do whatever I want, even stay out all night and never call home. I don't say I was away on a trip, traveling under the influence of LSD. At his wits end with my witless attitude and bad behavior, Dad grabs a big handful of my long hair and threatens legal action, warning he'll take me to court and have the judge place me in state custody, an alarming maneuver and announcement. Luckily, Mom steps in before Dad decides to knock some sense into his impudent sixteen-year-old son. But he already has my full attention. His emergency response has shocked my heart back into its regular rhythm, reviving my dull conscience and soon our anesthetized relationship. I'm aware again and concerned now that my inconsiderate conduct caused a nightlong nightmare for my parents.

Within the hour, Dad and I end up alone in the kitchen, face-to-face in front of the stove, a few feet away from where the cosmic egg exploded. I suppose that he sought me out, that he initiated what only looks like a chance encounter, probably after talking with Mom. We're both truly sorry about what happened earlier and once we stand close and look each other in the eye, our months-long animosity finally melts. We exchange heartfelt apologies, and that prompts an impromptu muscular embrace. Actually saying "I'm sorry" lets us let go of old wounds, and an uncommon embrace enables us to grab hold and hang on for our dear life, desperate to close the deadening distance. Magic words wave away hurt feelings and a magic gesture works its wonders. I feel an intense blend of grief and relief, sorrow and release, free now to begin to develop a budding desire to change my direction and find my own unique way forward.

Not long after, Dad suggests I apply for a fulltime position at IBM. You need a referral from a relative already on the payroll, and he works at the Poughkeepsie plant. Too weary and unsure of myself to fight this fate, I acquiesce for now and accept an offer to start in September on a ninety-day trial at the Fishkill plant. In the meantime, Sam Macy bought two tickets to the music festival that's happening across the Hudson River in mid-August, and he doesn't want to go alone. Actually, he's afraid to go alone, plus his protective mother probably won't let him go alone since he's only fifteen. I don't want to spend that much time in his annoying company or sleep overnight in a filthy field for two days, but I'd like to hear the music, so I agree to go as his guest. Then out of the blue he decides to take this cute girl with short black hair instead, a girl that I also liked before they began going out. And just like that, I'm SOL, shit out of luck, as my mother would say, disappointed but also relieved that I only almost went to Woodstock.

I'm already disillusioned with the counterculture anyway. It's nowhere near what I had hoped for, more about rejecting and withdrawing from society than about building a better world. Although it will be awhile before I stop puffing my water pipe in the privacy of my own home, I've already quit dropping acid. And I'm starting to see that the hippie movement's a lot like a bowel movement—it's good to get rid of all that old crap and flush it down the toilet, but it still stinks, and you have to wipe yourself when you're done or you'll smell like hell.

---

*The remainder of this paragraph consists largely of lines taken from the lyrics of Joni Mitchell's "Woodstock," quoted, paraphrased, and reordered. Siquomb Publishing Company.

Fledging

We tow our camping trailer up a long, steep hill, inching along toward High Point State Park, the engine overheating in the hot weather, Dad coaxing the rig upward, steady and easy on the gas; Mom and I alongside, likewise leaning forward on the edge of the wide front seat. We whine on and on and on, our breath suspended in the summer air, hoping to make it to our campsite before the car breaks down. We finally reach the highest point in New Jersey, peel our sticky bodies off the burning plastic interior, and climb out for our one-night stay. We've come from a Bestline business meeting, referred there by Louie and Marie Gagarono, our next-door neighbors on Myers Corners Road, back in Wappingers Falls; and we plan to return early tomorrow morning to hear more about how we might make money in a multilevel corporation that sells cleaning products. We're weary but still animated enough to stay up late, chattering about this opportunity to increase our income and improve our lives.

I've been working at IBM for nine months now, long enough to know that I don't want to stay stuck on an assembly line until

I receive the proverbial gold watch when I retire in almost fifty years. Dad knows I'm unhappy at IBM and dissatisfied with my prospects and he wants to hear my opinion, so he urged me to come on this business trip, inviting me along like an equal adult. We hear about an even more lucrative opportunity at the early morning executive meeting, but it requires a three-thousand-dollar cash investment, secured by five thousand dollars' worth of inventory. After the presentation, company representatives answer our questions and then give us time to talk about what we want to do. Would we rather just sell products as a local distributor and make maybe a few hundred dollars a month? Or do we want to become a direct distributor and later a general distributor and operate in more of a management capacity and possibly earn thousands of dollars per month part-time?

Dad looks at Mom and she says, "Whatever you want to do, Henry." He leans close in his quiet and confidential way and asks me what I think, like he really wants and needs to know where I stand, my attitude and outlook.

"What have we got to lose, let's go for it," I respond.

"You want to go in as partners or what?"

"Yeah, sure, that'd be great."

"What about the investment?"

I tell him I'll go fifty-fifty with him, doable since I save most of what I earn at IBM; I don't know how Dad raises his half. We fill out an application and agree that we'll work the business evenings and weekends. Mom and Dad sign the papers since I won't be eighteen for a few months. While we're waiting for our shipment to arrive, Dad confides that he's thinking of backing out and cancelling the contract because of financial concerns he doesn't fully describe. When he sees that I would feel let-down and disheartened and that I want to forge ahead, he decides to dismiss his second thoughts and stand pat, conceding my point that the business might help alleviate the difficulties. I never know if Dad feels encouraged by my naïve confidence or if he simply sacrifices his fears for my benefit, despite his misgivings.

As bad timing would have it, I'm away on vacation when our order arrives and unable to help lift and lug and stack dozens of cases of cleaning products floor to ceiling in our now bulging basement, hundreds of pounds of potential profits. I'm off touring upstate New York with Joe Mubarek, my best buddy and our close family friend, home on leave after a tour of duty at an Air Force base in Turkey, where he says the toilet paper sports large splinters. We enjoy a truly edifying trip, traveling through one of the most amazing areas on earth, catching up yet keeping quiet most of the time, listening to the multicolored landscape with our eyes; mindful of the mighty Saint Lawrence Seaway; absorbed in its heavily-forested and lightly-inhabited Thousand Islands, eighteen-hundred little homelands that look like living buoys in the wide channel, safe from the outside world. I only wish that we had time to drive the entire length of the watercourse that connects the Great Lakes to the Atlantic Ocean, three hundred and seventy miles of scenic countryside.

While Joe was far away playing government-sponsored spy games, monitoring the radio transmissions of Soviet fighter pilots as a full-fledged adult, I've been moving toward maturity here at home, in the land of the we-wish-we-were truly free and the home of the we-wish-we-were really brave; fully free from fear and from want and free to worship and to speak our minds without being watched by Big Brother; and brave enough to leave our empty jobs behind and strike out on our own. Lately I've been learning about being part of the mindless adult grind; about how it really feels to eke out a living in an increasingly industrialized society where everything imaginable is up for sale, where even human beings are bought and sold for the lowest possible prices on the so-called labor market.

I'm already bored out of my gourd on the IBM assembly line, a little cog in a big wheel, performing the same repetitive tasks forty hours a week plus plenty of overtime—and some of the other workers have been going for decades, now nearly meshed with the machinery. I earn enough for what I want and need for now and to contribute my fair share at home, but I don't find a real sense of satisfaction or authentic craft in my meaningless labors. And fifty-six to sixty-two-hour workweeks mean more money, but they also mean I don't have enough time for other activities or see much sun in the winter months. Fortunately, the machine I operate is ingeniously designed to provide frequent unplanned breaks from this mountain of monotony. It hangs up so often—crushing the parts rather than printing a number on top—that we stop every few minutes to clear the track, a riskier but less tedious task. We stop, unblock the jam, and start again, and again, and yet again. We repeat the routine with mounting irritation until the little monster decides to cooperate or until we throw up our hands and call in the experts. We scream what's wrong to our department technicians amid the incessant sound emanating from a roomful of these roaring contraptions.

At the end of each shift, we give the little monster his daily bath and then we wash our hands to go home. Unfortunately, it's impossible—especially if you're brand new and assigned a bad machine—not to stain your fingers with indelible ink, and we scrub it all off with alcohol and Scotch-Brite pads made for inanimate pots and pans. No wonder my fingers are dried-out and split-open, but the cracks make a nice natural channel for the alcohol when it's time to wash up again tomorrow.

What I like best about working at IBM is getting to know nice people, people different from those I've known all my life, like Nan, the first Black person I've ever befriended, and Bill, both believing and practicing Protestants. We need to yell to talk—except during lunch, when it's dead quiet—but at least I don't have to scrub the skin off my fingers and pour alcohol on the open wounds afterwards. And there aren't many jams in our conversations, none with Nan, and all easily cleared without the aid of any of our technicians. I mostly listen to Nan talk about her challenges, and I try to affirm her feelings and attitudes. She quietly mentions her marriage and her young children and her unfaithful husband and expresses her firm, matter-of-fact faith in doing what she knows is right and in being faithful, her belief that things will work out in God's own way. I'm sorry about her situation, but I'm impressed with her courage and commitment.

Bill's in his early twenties and engaged to be married, nervous and excited but talking like a responsible young adult preparing to establish his own household, all new to me since I don't have older brothers. But we talk mostly about life's big questions and about religion, because he's eager to share his Baptist faith and I'm willing to seek insight and answers whatever the source and wherever it leads. He says I sound like someone that knows the Bible, and I say he sounds like someone that has experienced drugs, so we agree on an exchange of more than ideas—I agree to read portions of the Bible for the first time and he accepts an invitation to smoke marijuana for the first time. I'm surprised when he consents so willingly; I don't know how he feels about my ready response.

One evening after work, Bill comes over to my house and we head downstairs to my psychedelic den, where we turn on the music and light and pass the water pipe. Since he's a first-timer, it takes a lot for him to get high, so this experiment costs me a lot more precious contraband than I expected. Worse yet, Bill makes me paranoid and uncomfortable, looking and pointing and laughing at me, acting like an idiot and encroaching on my mental, emotional, and personal space. I tell him again and again to please knock it off, but he finds that funny, rich fodder for his mirthful mood, a cause for more mocking and staring and giggling. Now I remember why I always prefer getting high by myself—and why I wanted to share the experience with Bill to begin with, why in my mind it's analogous to his interest in religion and his invitation to read the Bible. For me this is more than a form of recreation, just a way to have a good time—it's a meaningful spiritual practice, a type of personal meditation. I'm looking for enlightenment, not laughter, and Bill's irreverent; he doesn't get it, and I'm disillusioned.

I'm glad Bill never offered to read the Bible with me, that I'm free to wander in on my own and at my leisure. I read parts of Genesis and then peruse portions of other books I find fairly accessible and also interesting: Proverbs, Psalms, Job, Ezekiel, and especially the gospels of Matthew, Mark, Luke, and John. I read with belief in the Bible's divine origin, and I experience a peaceful power and a subtle sense of truth. I now believe more than ever in the existence of God and on a more solid and more informed footing.

After two separate ninety-day contracts at IBM, I'm eligible to be hired as a permanent employee, but there's a problem. Permanent employees start out on the graveyard shift, and I'm still only seventeen, under the legal age for shiftwork. But my manager recommends that the company make an exception and allow me to stay on the dayshift since I'm an excellent worker. Unfortunately, this means I must move to another department, to the print shop, where I'm unhappy with the work and also with my coworkers, who tease and humiliate me, damaging my dignity and self-respect.

My new department rarely requires overtime and that means less money and too many hours alone since I seldom see my former friends anymore. I'm on my own again during most of my leisure time—except when I play chess with my younger brothers and my new brother-in-law—only now it's not comic books and model cars. It's listening to music on my expensive new stereo system, playing the beautiful Gibson electric bass guitar I bought, reading from the Bible and other books, and thinking, just really thinking about things. My lonely, empty life leads me to seek comfort and to look for light. I ponder and I even pray. But rather than just repeat formal, set prayers like I learned as a child, I carry on truly earnest conversations with God in my mind. Now and again, I actually utter my agonies out loud, even kneel down on occasion, my face in my pillow for privacy. After six miserable months in the new department, I decide to quit and free myself from this unpleasant prison. I figure that we're off to a good start in the Bestline business and I could do it fulltime now. Dad doesn't say much at all, just "if that's what you really want to do," but I believe he thinks that it's probably a premature step. I don't want to disappoint him, but I just can't suffer at IBM any longer.

I don't know very many people and inviting former passing acquaintances to our recruiting meetings makes me anxious and panicky, so there's a definite downside, but Bestline still opens up a wonderful new world. It's more about building a lifestyle than merely making a living, about developing character as well as earning money, about helping out other people as much as meeting your own goals, about what the company calls true "growth into greatness," about integrity, courage, compassion, hard work, and spirituality. And that's what happens over the next two years—I build a better life and a better self, although I don't make much money at all. I change from an insecure and withdrawn almost eighteen-year-old factory worker to a more confident and more outgoing nearly twenty-year-old business leader that provides corporate training and makes presentations in public recruiting meetings. In the process, I gain the respect of the more mature members of our group, who admire how advanced and articulate I am at my young age and marvel at my ability to inspire others to action, to call them to consciously consider what they truly want.

I also make friends with good people who seek a better and more meaningful life, people that celebrate your successes and sympathize with your setbacks, both in the business and in everyday life, a genuine community of colleagues. My parents and I grow especially close to Jack Hunt, a sharp young adult my Dad knew at IBM, and to two young families with kids in elementary school, Marco and Charlene Fernandez and John and Shelley Zanavone. John eventually becomes my first fully-adult friend with a family, giving me a glimpse into what my own life might look like in ten years, with a nice wife, four sweet children, and a three-bedroom house. I also see the pressure he feels to provide a more abundant living, his deep desire to meet their many growing needs, now and as the future unfolds.

When John, now our area leader, leaves his day job at IBM to work at Bestline fulltime, the company assigns him to open up some new areas around the Hudson Valley, an opportunity and a burden. But it takes two people to put on a recruiting meeting, and John doesn't want to go it alone anyway, so he asks me to work with him, a real honor. I wonder if Dad put the bug in his ear, telling John that I'm available since I'm no longer employed at IBM. Our attempts to open other towns are unsuccessful, but we gain one another's company and become good friends, and John and Shelley appreciate my support—and I feel more like a full-fledged adult.

Soon after his discharge from the Air Force, my old buddy Joe Mubarek joins our Bestline organization, and he and Jack Hunt and I become the three musketeers of positive thinking and living. We form a small study group devoted to developing mental and moral discipline and spend our spare time listening to tapes by Earl Nightingale and by Bestline founder William E. Bailey; reading from *Think and Grow Rich* and *As a Man Thinketh*; discussing the ideas and encouraging one another to strive for continual self-improvement.

As I become more involved in Bestline, I begin to experience elements of what I once sought in the sixties counterculture— an opportunity to develop sustainable spirituality and to create genuine community, ways to participate in society without being overcome by worldly habits. I eventually decide this higher road won't take me to my ultimate destination after all—but in the meantime it takes me to the trailhead that leads to the narrow path I still follow today, more than four decades later.

Close Encounters

"How's your mental health?"

"Fine," I mutter, startled and also humiliated by Mr. Pruitt's impertinent question—he's been pleasant enough until now. And sociable enough last Friday when he attended a Bestline recruiting meeting to learn about a business opportunity I want to share; even though he decided that he'd rather discuss the details over lunch today than return for the Saturday morning executive session when we try to persuade our prospects to invest and become direct distributors. But Mr. Pruitt has misled me. He isn't interested in hearing more about the business, and our congenial conversation shifts abruptly when he asks about my emotional stability. I guess my former high school guidance counselor thinks I'm unstable because I was so bored in Miss Prissy's history class that I almost failed to graduate three years ago. Talk about clomping to conclusions.

But Mr. Pruitt's tactless question is only light fare compared to the bulk of our distasteful dialogue—a philosophical dispute about freedom of choice in education and career. I argue for individual agency, for our right to decide our own destiny at every turn and to change our choices at any time, even if it hampers the efficiency of the state or adversely effects the general welfare. Mr. Pruitt insists on complete state control, claiming the government should evaluate each citizen's abilities in light of society's needs and then dictate a person's training and occupation once and for all, denying any opportunity to alter direction as the future unfolds.

At first I naïvely assume that this is an amiable argument, an exercise to explore the topic, a teacher attempting to challenge a student's thinking, that Mr. Pruitt is simply playing the devil's advocate. But I soon see that he's dead serious, that he fully and fanatically espouses these extreme beliefs, and that his attacks are intended to crush me—my mind and my heart and my spirit, not just my position on this issue. I'm certain in my soul that there's something very sick and wrong with his outlandish outlook, that coercion is ultimately unjust and immoral. But I lack his advanced education and I'm unable to answer his well-articulated arguments or fend off his zealous assaults. I'm out of gas and he's roaring in high gear, expelling the noxious fumes of his dogmatic doctrine, polluting the atmosphere and poisoning my mind and heart.

I feel physically ill, my light lunch flip-flopping in my upset stomach, my mind swimming in a dismal swamp of increasing confusion, muddled and alarmed. And then the real horror hits me hard. I gaze into Mr. Pruitt's furious face and he looks like a zombie, his pupils and irises absent, his eyes devoid of light, the sure sign of intelligent life. This is just barely a sentient being. I detect an angry darkness, a vile, unfamiliar evil emanating from his unfeeling form, and I'm afraid, the fear invading my body, seeping toward the center of my soul. I need to leave—now. I also sense a supportive presence lending me the strength and the courage to end this awful confrontation with a respectable public servant transformed into a dreadful monster. I cut off my conversation with Dr. Jekyll-cum-Mr. Hyde and stand up and dismiss myself and turn and walk away, striding toward the door and out into the sunlight and fresh air. I slide into our familiar family car, a lightly used '69 Lincoln Continental Coupe my parents bought to impress business prospects, a car that I wash and polish and clean and vacuum—a car that now sustains and comforts me, the firm dark-green, tucked-and-rolled leather seat a safe place, like a leather couch in a cozy den.

I'm haunted by this odd and unexpected encounter with evil for several days and want to tell someone what happened. But I need an amicable ear, somebody that will hear what's in my heart and on my mind, that won't dismiss the event or minimize my reaction or question my mental health. And then one day I'm standing in the kitchen with my best friend, Joe Mubarek, next to the sink where the cosmic egg exploded. My parents' long-standing financial problems have at last led the bank to foreclose on their mortgage, and we need to vacate the house on Myers Corners Road. I'm about to lose my longtime home and Joe his home away from home. And this is likely our last time together here in the heart of this house, where for years we joked and laughed and told stories and talked until late at night.

Our conversation glides easily into an earnest and reflective groove, and I decide to tell Joe about what happened with Mr. Pruitt. We explore the implications of the incident and share profound feelings about God, our beliefs and questions about his plans and his purposes. We yearn for truth as we attempt to articulate our limited understanding of the purposes of life. And an intelligence beyond our own is made manifest during our exchange, enabling us to achieve a small measure of insight, yet leaving us mindful that we lack solid knowledge. At this point, an absolutely hyperreal essence fills the room, permeating our bodies and enlightening our minds with an awed awareness that we are not alone. We are overcome, unable to speak, immersed in a condensed atmosphere—I can almost see the air. The fully palpable presence thickens and swells within the surrounding silence, increasing in intensity. My feet feel like they're floating off the floor, and my head feels farther from my feet than usual, as though I'm taller, closer to the ceiling. Joe and I gaze at one another for what seems like a long time. We both know that there's a divine presence come into the kitchen, that God has graciously intervened in our little ordinary lives—to endorse our efforts, to encourage us to continue our search, and to hold out hope that our labors will eventually bear abundant fruit.

Hoping to find our answers in an organized religion whose teachings address our questions, Joe and I decide to search for a church, to visit a different denomination each week until we find one we want to join. To scout out the possibilities, we look in the local newspaper for times and places. But before we can attend any meetings, Marco and Charlene Fernandez stand up at a Bestline social one evening and share what's happening in their business and their personal lives. And Charlene mentions that they've recently returned from a trip to a beautiful temple in Salt Lake City, where they participated in sacred ceremonies and were married for eternity. Curious, my mother and I each talk with Charlene and Marco for just a few minutes afterwards about their church—The Church of Jesus Christ of Latter-day Saints; and a few weeks later two missionaries stop by our new apartment and meet my parents, who are just about to leave and ask them to return on another day.

Rolling Ridge

We've left behind our longtime home on Myers Corners Road, but I find Rolling Ridge Apartments pleasant enough, especially now that I'm nineteen and spending more time indoors these days, daydreaming about success in the Bestline business. I'm puttering around one summer evening, making myself at ease in my new bedroom, when Mom calls for me to come downstairs. I'm surprised when two neatly-trimmed young adults, wearing a charcoal gray and a dark blue suit and white shirts and plain ties, shake my hand and introduce themselves. And I'm puzzled— they're both named Elder, a name I've never heard before. They explain that elder is their title, but I'm confused again when one elder says that his first name is Eldon, blurring his unfamiliar title with his unusual name, making him Elder Eldon Taylor, a muddling mouthful. Still I'm impressed: we're about the same age, but they're as mature and confident as I wish I were.

We sit down in our new living room and Elder Taylor talks to my parents while Elder Christensen speaks with me, leaning in so I can hear, rather than raising his voice, as if he's sharing a confidential message. I try to hear both conversations but listen mainly to Elder Christensen. I can't say I fully grasp his quiet communiqué, but I like what he has to say, that they've come to tell us that the Lord has called a prophet in our day, that there's a living prophet on the earth again, and that the true Church of Jesus Christ has been restored. I'm intrigued and ask where the prophet lives, expecting him to name Palestine, but he says Salt Lake City. His answer seems strange yet reasonable. Picturing a bearded man in robes, leading a flock, I ask him what the living prophet looks like. He replies that he wears a suit, eyeglasses, and is clean shaven. Again his odd answer sounds logical—and it rings true. But I hide my excitement and continue my cross-examination, on guard against accepting his answers too easily. "What's his name?" I ask, expecting a biblical name like Isaiah or Ezekiel. "Harold B. Lee," he responds.

I'm surprised by Elder Christensen's straightforward replies and his matter-of-fact manner. I ponder and see a bearded man named Moses that I believe was a prophet thousands of years ago. I visualize a man in a suit in Salt Lake City, Utah, named Harold B. Lee, and it makes sense that a modern prophet would be just a normal person, as prophets were in olden days. I don't know quite how to react, so I press forward with more guarded skepticism. "How do I know that you're right about this?" I ask. "How can I know if what you say is true? How can I know if he's a prophet?" A challenge and a promise, Elder Christensen's answer leaves me lost in silent thought: "You can pray about it and you will know."

A few days later, the elders return and show us a filmstrip called "Man's Search for Happiness." It addresses the questions that I have hidden in my heart, the questions that Joe Mubarek and I raised in the kitchen of my family's house back on Myers Corners Road, questions about God's plans and purposes, and about the meaning of life. Where did we come from? Why are we here? And where are we going after we die? The narration affirms what I already believe, articulating my vague notions in clear and confident language. I recognize at once that what I'm hearing is true and that it's from God. I sense that this is what I have long been looking for, and I'm thrilled but unnerved by the unknown—an unforeseen future opening up before me, a straight and narrow path, a path unlike the road to riches that I'm presently pursuing.

I want to share the elders' fascinating message with my friend Joe Mubarek, but I also need to hear his opinion and to have his counsel and support. I report what they have said so far, and I then invite him to investigate along with me. He meets with the missionaries and then joins us for their first formal lesson—about the loss of gospel knowledge and of divine authority in ancient times and their subsequent restoration in these last days. The elders inform us that the fullness of the true gospel was lost after the death of the original twelve apostles, along with the divine power and authority they received from Jesus Christ; that the Father and the Son—glorified beings with bodies of flesh and bone—visited Joseph Smith in 1820 to initiate a restoration; and that a few years later, they sent heavenly messengers—John the Baptist and then Peter and James and John—to confer the priesthood on Joseph Smith, including the divine authority to organize the true Church of Jesus Christ and to perform valid baptisms and bestow the gift of the Holy Ghost.

The missionaries invite us to be baptized, and I agree that I will once I know for sure that their message is true. I'm excited about the possibility that I have found the proverbial pearl of great price, but I'm concerned about changing my entire life. I recognize that if I intend to act with integrity, I will be obliged to live according to the teachings of Christ and of his restored church. My life goes up in the air for the next few months, my purposes suspended until I know one way or another.

I'm not yet absolutely sure during the first few weeks, but when the elders talk to us, encouraging words echo in my mind: "It's true. Listen. It's right. Don't turn away. Pursue this. Keep going. Something truly wonderful is in store." And as they place paper cutouts on their flannel board as a visual aid, I experience an intense sense of déjà vu. I know this message. It's as much mine as theirs. I'm not learning, I'm remembering. When these feelings of familiarity come over me, I hardly hear the elders, their voices and their words merely background behind the more vivid voice I hear in my heart and the more prominent words I perceive in my mind. It's as if I'm in a trance, and yet I'm wide awake, more awake than ever before. I feel fully alive, my body warm and vibrant, elated and overjoyed, sensations I savor and crave.

On a later occasion, I feel a powerful divine presence as the elders place paper cutouts on the flannel board representing the different stages in the plan of salvation: our life as the literal spirit children of our Father in Heaven before we were born; birth and our mortal probationary period here on earth, during which we obtain our bodies of flesh and bone, repent of our wrongdoings, and learn to live by faith; death and the spirit world; the sacred atoning sacrifice of Jesus Christ that brings about our resurrection, permanently reuniting our spirits and our bodies, making us immortal; the judgment and the various kingdoms of glory where we will dwell in eternity as glorified resurrected beings. I stare at the flannel board and it almost looks alive, emanating light, the entire scene burning into my soul as absolutely real, as heavenly truth sent from God the Father. I feel like I'm floating in the midst of eternity, certain I have seen and heard this all before, some eternal time ago.

During another brief lesson, I sit in our living room with my parents, listening to the two elders recount how Joseph Smith received and translated the ancient record known as The Book of Mormon—a second witness, with the Bible, that Jesus Christ is the Son of God and the Savior of the world. I am amazed at their strange yet familiar message, as strangely familiar as their previous messages about modern-day prophets and apostles. I have never even heard about The Book of Mormon before, and here we are living in upstate New York, only a few hundred miles away from where the events they describe took place.

After hearing the missionaries' message, my father leaves the room for a few minutes. To our complete surprise, he returns holding an older copy of The Book of Mormon. He says that he picked it up at a hotel in Chicago while he was in the army toward the end of World War II. He hands it to me, his eldest son, insisting that I take it for my own. He seems to sense that a close acquaintance with this peculiar book will alter the course of my life, this simple gift his way to play a part in what he hopes will happen for me, to help me realize my new unfolding future. Over the next several weeks, I read the ancient record in earnest, praying with real intent to know if it is true. I eventually experience a profound conversion, a deep desire to repent and come unto Christ.

But the missionaries' lessons aren't all weighty doctrine and spiritual experiences. One day the elders are teaching a lesson on the Lord's law of physical health, placing their paper cutouts on the flannel board they have set up on the living room floor. Without warning, Trouble runs into the room, marches over to their flannel board, raises his left leg, and soaks several paper cutouts, which shrivel and fall to the floor. Mom grabs the little black terrier by his collar, puts him out, and apologizes. Elder Taylor's clearly displeased but holds his tongue, a fine display of discipline; after all, plenty of people would be pissed enough to pee their pants.

Several months later, another set of missionaries stop by for an informal visit, and they mention that there's a hilarious story going around the mission about a dog who peed on a flannel board during a lesson, soiling the flannel and ruining an elder's paper cutouts. We listen and laugh and then tell them it was our dog that did the dastardly deed. The elders are embarrassed and apologetic, but we're happy to hear that Trouble is the antihero in an anecdote now included in their repertoire of stories about bizarre missionary experiences.

We not only listen to missionary lessons, we also attend church meetings and social activities, where we meet ordinary members and lay leaders of the local congregation. Charlene and Marco Fernandez introduce us to people I find friendly and down-to-earth. I'm aware that there aren't any paid positions, yet I'm surprised that the bishop's just a regular guy, a chemical engineer at a local firm, kind and loving, with a warm smile, a person who puts you at ease in his presence—and that he wears no special vestments or regalia, only a suit, white shirt, and tie. I'm also impressed by the way ordinary members participate in sacrament meeting, even older children, and that they're humble and sincere, simple and grateful, enthusiastic and happy: leading the music, playing the organ, singing hymns, offering prayers, reading scriptures, and giving talks on gospel topics.

As we wait within the unadorned chapel for the sacrament meeting to begin, I feel enfolded within a warm, welcoming, and divine presence, a sensation that intensifies as the bread and water are blessed and passed to the congregation, emblems of the body and the blood of Christ. An almost audible impression envelops me, puts me at ease, and entices me to return: "You are home. This is where you belong. Welcome. Come again. I know that you're nervous, but don't turn away. This is it. This is what you've long been looking for. This is what you've always wanted. You've found it. This is my church, the true Church of Jesus Christ. I am here. Come, join my people. This is home. You've come home."

Too interested to relax and listen, I also appreciate Brother Sean Murray's Sunday school class for investigators, their weird word for people learning about the gospel and the church. A knowledgeable Scottish convert, he welcomes my many curious questions, providing frank and honest answers, showing me that the Church has nothing to hide. I learn more details about the restoration of the gospel and feel that now familiar sensation tickling the inside of my soul, buzzing my body and animating my spirit.

As our baptismal date approaches, Mom is ready, and also my good friend Joe Mubarek, but Dad hasn't been able to stop smoking—he started when he was only twelve. I continue to cultivate a deepening desire to prepare to truly receive the gift of the Holy Ghost, the heavenly power that will enable me to keep the sacred covenant that I must make—to follow Christ, to obey his commandment to love one another and to bear one another's burdens, to help and comfort those that stand in need.

I soon see that if I want to receive an unmistakable answer and experience a deep change, I must ask and act with a sincere heart, with real intent, having faith in Christ, that I must pray with a proper attitude and conduct myself in a more righteous manner. I conclude that if it's all true, it will be worth whatever changes that I must make to become a better person, a genuine disciple of Jesus Christ. And so I quietly repent and truly seek to sacrifice my sins, to make my actions more congruent with my newfound attitudes. The missionary lessons, church meetings, and my personal study of The Book of Mormon nourish my hungry soul, enabling me to sustain my good faith efforts to develop greater inner strength. I feast upon the word of God, reading and pondering and praying frequently and fervently.

Soon enough God grants me a great gift—he makes the truth known to me by the power of the Holy Ghost—not once but again and again and again. On one occasion, I retire to my room to read The Book of Mormon and to pray. Kneeling on the floor beside my bed, I ache for an answer as I cry out to God for forgiveness and for revelation. And I feel the room fill with a heavenly presence, the air electric, the floor alive beneath my knees, the walls weightless, the building suspended above the earth. I am moved to the marrow, my whole body on fire, the healing heat of heaven sanctifying my soul and enlightening my mind. I feel in my bones that it's all absolutely true. I know for myself without a doubt. Heavenly Father lives and loves us and answers our prayers. Jesus Christ is the literal Son of God and the Savior of the world and broke the bands of death. He lives and he loves us and atoned for our sins. Joseph Smith is indeed a true prophet, the instrument through whom Christ restored his gospel and his divine authority. And The Church of Jesus Christ of Latter-day Saints is the Lord's true and living church, led by a living prophet today.

Exactly one week after my twentieth birthday, I am baptized by immersion and given the gift of the Holy Ghost by the laying on of hands. Following an opening hymn and prayer and two talks, the baptism itself is over in a flash—a flash of heavenly light. I emerge from the font and return to the dressing room dripping wet in my heavy white jumpsuit, feeling clean to the core, body and soul. I look into the mirror, expecting to see a clear complexion. I examine my face, surprised to find the same old blemishes but amazed to know my spirit is spotless. I feel free, the weight of sin washed away. I change my clothes and return to the chapel, ready to receive the gift of the Holy Ghost.

Now that I have been born of the water and of the spirit, I see that I have actually entered in at the gate and passed into a completely new sphere of existence. I feel awake and aware and able to see things as they really are, able to see that this is the kingdom of God on earth, and able to interpret the scriptures and to understand the gospel. I feel a sincere concern for others and a deep desire to serve them. I also feel grateful for Heavenly Father's loving and welcoming arms around me and for the heartfelt affection of fellow members, especially a nice group of other recent young adult converts. Joe Mubarek has also joined the Church, of course, and Jack Hunt, our friend from Bestline, will soon also become converted to the restored gospel. There aren't many members of the Church in the area, so we form a fairly close-knit community, along with several families that are raising young children and teenagers. I later find that this isn't necessarily the case in other places where I live later in life, but for now my quest for community, begun during my years in the counterculture and then continued in Bestline, along with my desire to commune with God, has been abundantly satisfied.

~*~

I'm far too naïve at first to know that I'm still full of faults, that I have a long history to overcome, that I will make many mistakes as I mature to full manhood. I'm too much a neophyte to fully appreciate an essential purpose of mortal life—to learn and to grow from everyday experiences, from confronting the challenges of earthly existence, developing the discipline and the character that will eventually enable me to enjoy eternal life.

In the decades to come, I will learn that being a disciple of Christ doesn't mean a trouble-free life. I will have a lifetime to learn that it doesn't exempt me and especially my loved ones, my wife and my children and my aging parents, from ill health, including cancers and strokes; from many decades of inadequate employment; from chronic marital troubles; from having a little girl with a very rare and potentially life-threatening illness; two daughters seriously injured in an auto accident; twin sons born seven weeks premature, one weighing less than three pounds; and children that struggle with allergies and eating disorders and drug and alcohol addiction and mental illness; and one son that endures overdoses, attempts suicide, and violates the law, that lives on the streets and in shelters and spends time in hospitals and treatment centers and in the county jail and the state prison.

But I will also have a lifetime to learn that when I make an honest effort to follow his example in good faith, and to draw upon his power, being a disciple of Jesus Christ does make a major difference; that his teachings and atonement enable me to see things in proper perspective and to respond in healthy ways, and they give me the opportunity to make corrections when I mishandle what happens. And I will have a lifetime to learn that the gifts of his gospel enable me to love others, to enjoy and to remember precious family moments and members, to serve by doing worthwhile and careful work, and to experience beauty.

After wandering in this wilderness for more than forty years beyond my baptism, moving slowly toward the promised land, traveling through this dark and dreary waste, looking for a city that has foundations, whose builder and maker is God, I know that to always retain the name of Christ written upon my heart is no superficial or easy matter; that whenever I forget to always remember him, life is much more likely to leave me looking like something the cat dragged through the keyhole on a rainy night, as my mother would say; but that when I am mindful and make the Prince of Peace my master, I am comforted in the midst of turmoil and made free from fear, liberated by faith.

Myers Corners Road

God's country. I'm back in God's country, back where I first felt that mysterious palpable presence, in the sky and clouds, in the hills and woods, in the rocks and trees, in the ponds and lakes, in the streams and rivers and waterfalls, in the pheasants and frogs, in the deer and rabbits, in the cows and chickens, in the farms and orchards. After eleven eventful years away from this heavenly landscape that continues to call me homeward, I've returned to the pastoral Hudson Valley. I'm back in the pleasant, peaceful place where I grew up, the wild place where I awakened, where I first felt the creative energy of the earth, where I first heard her humming, crying, sighing, singing songs of sorrow and joy, of loneliness and love, death and life. I'm back where my attitudes took root, where my values found form, where my body, mind, heart, and soul began to grow and to take shape, back where I experienced the influential events that formed a vital episode in my early life on earth.

Now a returning pilgrim playing tour guide for my wife, I drive down Myers Corners Road, eyeing places from my past, places that I haven't seen since '73, since my family moved away a few months before I turned twenty-one. We're celebrating our sixth anniversary, our two daughters in the care of a dear friend at home in New Haven, where we've lived since '82. We're on our way to Woodstock for the weekend, and we want to see the sights and scenes where I grew up—the house that Dad built, the neighborhood and nearby ponds and apple orchards, Roy C. Ketchum Senior High School, and the two-hundred-year-old farmhouse and my dear Wagon Wheel Delicatessen. I'm awed by the mysterious workings of time, by its magical, motionless movements, by what has changed in my absence and by what remains the same. The twisted section of Old Myers Corners Road where Mom ran into the barbed-wire fence that borders the apple orchard, still hidden from the outside world, and still no commemorative plaque in memory of Mom's mishap. The volunteer firehouse still stands silent at the intersection with All Angels Hill Road, witness of what happened on that rainy night when a foolish middle-aged man messed with Donna. The little country restaurant that made the tasty rotisserie chicken turned wholesale outlet for business machines, the maple tree Dad and I planted in the front yard grown from a tiny sapling to a large shade tree, the big carport transformed into a two-car garage.

We pull over onto the shoulder and see next to nothing—only a slab of cement encircled by weeds—where once upon a time the Wagon Wheel Delicatessen was a living and important place. Surprised and subdued, we knock on the front door of the old farmhouse to appeal for permission to amble around the large wooded lot; perhaps, we hope, they will invite us in when I explain that I once lived in this house. But the unsympathetic occupant shakes his head and warns us away. "There's nothing but snakes back there now," he says, turning around and quickly closing himself inside. I guess we should have knocked instead at the house Dad built long ago—they might have welcomed us home—but my mood felt less outgoing in that fleeting moment.

I'm startled by the distance between then and now, between Myers Corners Road and New Haven, Connecticut, and by the difference between who I was when we moved away and who I am today in 1984, a thirty-two-year-old husband and father and doctoral student at Yale University. I sense inside my soul the boy that here became a confused adolescent that developed into a newborn baby adult, young and yearning. But now I know he dwells within an older, wiser, and more experienced me, part of the many events that have inhabited these intervening years—a third of my entire lifetime and as long as I lived in this always precious place.

~*~

Tour guide again several decades later, I move slowly down Myers Corners Road once more, only today I'm in the congenial company of my daughter, Leah, a happily-married homemaker and the mother of three young children. But we aren't in a car; we're traveling on the Internet, surveying our surroundings via interactive satellite transmission, looking down from outer space and out at the screen, our bodies above and beyond the living place, far away from the physical reality of the beautiful Hudson Valley. And yet we're still able to view from a virtual distance realistic images of a place that she's never been before and that I haven't seen since '84, for nearly thirty long years, almost all of Leah's still young lifetime; long enough for Myers Corners Road to become a place I visit only in my mind and in my memories, the tangible place that once flowed through and all around me, embracing my body and animating my mind and heart and soul, now strangely absent from this palpable present.

For I inhabited that place during a particular time, and half a century separates then from now, the nine-year-old youngster from the fifty-nine-year-old grandfather. And yet Myers Corners Road continues, even the Myers Corners Road of my younger years—still out there, largely unchanged, and still here, in this present moment, truly bone of my bones and flesh of my flesh, an integral part of my mind and my emotions, of my very soul, informing who and what I am, son of the '60s and child of the heavenly Hudson Valley. For in the end, Myers Corners Road and I are one, and thus am I able to return whenever conditions are conducive, to travel to that then and there, and to conjure— by means of magic inherited from dear, departed parents—a portal through which others may also pass into that storied time and place.

Thanks

I thank my mother and father, Henry and Eileen Buonforte, for their wit and wisdom, for their patient support throughout my life, especially back when I was still growing up, for their stories and sayings, for the lessons their lives embodied, for the way they worked together through thick and thin and thinner. I also thank my older sister, Donna, and my younger brothers, Robert, Henry, and Kenneth, with whom I shared my younger years on Myers Corners Road. I thank the friends and the associates that appear in my memoir, for mingling their lives with mine, their privacy protected by pseudonyms. I thank my many students for their sincere interest and encouragement, and my dear friend Adam Lamoreaux for his enthusiastic support. I thank my sister Donna for her help with "Voodoo Juju" and "Don't Mess with Donna." Special thanks to my friend, able assistant, and wise advisor, Brynna Nelson, for her sharp eye, keen mind, and kind heart; her help has been vital and invaluable. Last but foremost, I thank my dear children, Leah, Christena, Nicholas, and James, and my grandchildren, for inspiring in me a desire to leave them this little legacy from my early life on earth.

About the Author

The grateful father of four and the grandfather of nine lively, creative, and beautiful human beings, writer Richard Buonforte (bone-FORT) lives on an island in the sky, where he likes to consider the clouds, look out at the lake, and watch the sun set and the moon rise over the mountains. He enjoys walking in the woods, encounters with wild animals, stimulating conversation, laughing out loud, listening to music, watching foreign films and live theater, cooking, playing tennis, and making music with the electric bass guitar. An award-winning teacher, he holds two advanced degrees from Yale and teaches at a respected private university in the Intermountain West. His favorite courses focus on American culture, memoir, and the importance of place in human experience.

Made in the USA
San Bernardino, CA
09 December 2017